Reconnaissance

Reconnaissance

on an educational frontier

R. A. HODGKIN

OXFORD UNIVERSITY PRESS
1970

Oxford University Press, Ely House, London W. 1

GLASGOW NEW YORK TORONTO MELBOURNE WELLINGTON
CAPE TOWN SALISBURY IBADAN NAIROBI DAR ES SALAAM LUSAKA
ADDIS ABABA BOMBAY CALCUTTA MADRAS KARACHI LAHORE DACCA
KUALA LUMPUR SINGAPORE HONG KONG TOKYO

Diagrams prepared by Brian and Constance Dear

PRINTED IN GREAT BRITAIN

TO ELIZABETH HODGKIN

Acknowledgements

I wish to thank many friends—colleagues and children—especially at Abbotsholme School and in the Sudan, who have taught me about education. Several major authorities deserve special acknowledgement for key quotations and for their ideas which have been used in this book, particularly Professors Susanne Langer of Connecticut College, Michael Polanyi of Oxford, and Donald MacKay of Keele. The last named and Professor W. H. Thorpe of Cambridge kindly read Chapters 7, 8, and 9 and made corrections and suggestions. There are others to whom I am indebted, like Jean Pierre Greenlaw at Bakht er Ruda for giving me a copy of *Philosophy in a New Key*, Professor Marjorie Grene for introducing me to *Personal Knowledge*, more recently Adam Hodgkin for the Waismann paper and Ian House for Vygotsky's book. Thanks are also due to several friends who were both severe and kind in their comments on a forerunner of this book which never appeared.

Chapter 10 appeared in slightly different form in the January 1969 number of *Trends in Education* published by the Department of Education and Science.

Contents

ALASSIO

This tree
Whose twist, whose angled thrust
Holds many ancient choices,
Rumours of voices
Past.

Dumb:
It seems to carry all the shape of years
Yet to forget the works that bent it.
They would have sounded in *our* ears
Like distant gales of words.

A stone (coal?)
Black and alone
Lies bedded in the root;
A common treasure
Mediating earth to air perhaps.
Or just quiet
At the tree's, the earth's
Still centre.

(*Round a Dream and Olive Trees, 1963*)

1 The frontier

Before Columbus set sail for America, he had dreamt of the Far East, and of the round world, and of the trackless ocean. Adventure rarely reaches its predetermined end. Columbus never reached China. But he discovered America. . . . Given the vigour of adventure, sooner or later the imagination reaches beyond the limits of the epoch.

ALFRED NORTH WHITEHEAD, *Adventures of Ideas*[1]

When we are involved in education, either as learners or teachers, there come moments when we see a new possibility or a new pattern. These may never be spectacular revelations, but when they occur, we share, in small measure, the experience of Columbus and Newton. We share a crumb with saints and artists. These moments happen when we enlarge our understanding, not by adding one more fact to the others but by developing the system in which all facts are lodged. This is conceptual growth. These are the small, irreversible explorations which make education come alive.

This book is about such individual enlargement. Many specialist disciplines throw light on the process. Teachers and parents have a privileged but unspecialized viewpoint, for they can know the process from within, as participants. Even with such experience, however, we need the technical language of specialists if we are to develop and communicate our understanding. We follow the philosophers some way into the pastures of epistemology and get from them an inkling of the meaning of 'knowledge'; the physicists and physiologists and psychologists present us with facts about communication and memory; we listen with more or less attention to anthropologists and sociologists and even to theologians. In the future perhaps some great thinker will emerge, a new Aristotle or Aquinas, who will synthesize these in one great

[1] Details of books mentioned are in the Bibliography, p. 100.

system, and our children will be wiser and, for a season, more confident than we are.

My aim is reconnaissance and questioning near the crucial zone which I shall call 'the frontier'. This means more than the common phrase, 'the frontiers of human achievement'—more and less. It is more commonplace yet often overlooked. Teachers frequently find themselves standing with one foot on this frontier, or watching someone else there. It can be reached in the classroom, though a school corridor, a workshop, or an expedition to the hills offers more promising conditions for discovering what education is really about.

What sort of process is this advance to the frontier where novelty breaks through? What sort of thing happens to people in ordinary situations—in discussion, in fantasy, in skilled action, through symbols, through works of art or worship? What common ground is there to these? What occurs when people gain insight and a strong desire to explore?

Let us assume that you—a teacher or parent—are watching a small boy, John, aged 10, as he paints a picture. His actions were triggered off by the mistress who teaches him. She said a few words, with Blake in mind, about eyes burning in the jungle and then produced trays of poster paints. Now we can see John's work on paper. It shows the side view of a gangling leopard, with large black spots, pushing through oval leaves. What John is doing is to make a representation of an image which has already formed in his mind. What results on paper is a compromise between various limitations of material and skill and this eidetic image that he 'sees' in his mind's eye.[2]

There are two possible ways in which you might be observing this scene. You might be doing research on the psychological significance of such painting. Your aim would then be objectivity and comparison; would you not be better further off, or even hidden behind a one-way mirror? You select and standardize the questions you ask about John's background and home. You

[2] Herbert Read, *Education Through Art*. Chapters 9 and 10 are especially relevant. For an account of experimental work in this field see Ralph Norman Haber, 'Eidetic Images', *Scientific American*, April 1969.

are preparing to 'place' his picture for comparison and classification in a range of other works by ten-year-olds. This is a perfectly good approach and if skilfully pursued it may yield valuable results. Nevertheless it is in marked contrast to the viewpoint and approach of an effective teacher.

Imagine now that you are seeing the situation as John's teacher would. She will want to be in touch with all her pupils, yet not too obviously with any one of them. She has not merely provided the materials and initial stimulus, she will also react, admiring a little, questioning, suggesting. She will compare John's leopard, mentally, with the beasts that other children have painted, but she also has the opportunity to place it in a category of which she has unique understanding. She can see it as one picture in a series which stretches through time, John's time, an evolving sequence, spanning the years she has known him and which points questioningly to the future. This is the subjective viewpoint which will be of special interest to us; but it does not exclude the other.[3]

In practice of course the experienced teacher is far from constant in his viewpoint. He swings from a position of relative detachment and objectivity to one of involvement and subjectivity. Both are important. But it is in the periods of subjective involvement, when teacher and child share something, that the most effective educational work is done. The actual moment of a child's illumination may come when he is alone. Nevertheless it is between pairs or in small groups, who share an aim or a question, that fruitful insights are most often generated.

In the next chapter we shall examine the existential and mutual nature of such encounters and shall then consider the need for balance and interplay between these and more objective, analytic views. But it is not only in twos and threes that progress towards the frontier is made. Sometimes an atmosphere of readiness and searching questions can pervade a whole class.

On one such occasion at Abbotsholme we were having a

[3] P. F. Strawson describes this complementary attitude in his essay 'Freedom and Resentment'. He points out that the treatment of children by parents 'must represent a kind of compromise constantly shifting in one direction, between objectivity . . . and developed human attitudes'. From *Studies in the Philosophy of Thought and Action* (p. 90).

seminar on drugs and alcohol. There were two visiting psychiatrists, a clergyman, five teachers, and fifty sixth-formers. Discussion turned particularly round L.S.D. The ideas and words which we used came from science, religion, philosophy, psychology, and from the ordinary experiences of school life. These all seemed to mix well in the arena of controversy. As long as we maintain a critical regard for truth there is much to be said for bringing together words and concepts unfamiliar with each other, from different realms of thought. This illustrates Koestler's idea[4] that when we allow normally divergent planes of association to intersect, original, illuminating, and sometimes humorous ideas may be generated. We might accept his view that this *bi-sociation*, as he terms it, is very often, perhaps always, related to creative advance.

Certainly the reasoning which emerged from our seminar was not narrowly scientific, nor sociological, nor aesthetic, nor religious—in the ordinary sense of the word. One boy drew a parallel between the heightened sensibility produced by L.S.D. and the aesthetic awareness which he had experienced when climbing mountains. Then the woman psychiatrist extended this and likened the experience and stamina of a mystic to those of a skilled mountaineer. The dabbler in L.S.D. then began to seem—we were not quite sure of the image—like someone in gym shoes on a glacier or like a fat man going to the top by *téléférique*, someone whose aim was kicks without competence. Gradually our ideas were centring on a large unformulated concept of what a man might become and the need for integrity and good workmanship and not taking too many short cuts, and then, when someone mentioned possible health dangers, this seemed important but not nearly as important as the concept of biological and spiritual wholeness which we seemed to be on the verge of understanding. Very few of these ideas were stated explicitly and for such a teaching situation this was just as well. It is easy for an adult in a large group, when discussing such subjects, to become an unwitting propagandist.

[4] Arthur Koestler, *Insight and Outlook*. He later developed the theme in *The Act of Creation*.

Does this rambling schoolboy discussion sound homespun? Perhaps, but this is inevitable when people are trying to shape their own values from diverse desires, concepts, and experiences. It is a central task of teachers to lead people to the possibility— the necessity, that each one learns as a maker or as an artist does, from the conflicts and complexities which exist inside a problem. For these are frontier situations where each person must feel and think existentially and then risk responsible action.

2 Inside knowledge

The first man of science was he who looked into a thing, not to learn whether it could furnish him with food, or shelter, or weapons, or tools, or ornaments, or *playwiths*, but he who sought to know it for the gratification of *knowing*; while he that first sought to *know* in order to *be* was the first philosopher.

COLERIDGE, from *Anima Poetae*

The art teacher is watching John struggling to paint the spots on the leopard. She may know that he could quite easily use his brush more effectively. He could twist it gently as he paints, so disciplining the wayward hairs which smudge the edges of each spot. But she knows that in some situations it is better not to give advice. Even if John is looking exasperated and is ready for help, she will be wise not to be too emphatic or to suggest more than an experiment. 'Why not try twisting that brush?' she will say before she moves on to the next jungle scene.

This attitude might be described as showing a proper respect for John's individual personality. But where does respect fit into this small piece of original exploration? For one thing this attitude or non-interference acknowledges that John should be left free and, therefore, in a sense solitary, as he explores a small sector of his private conceptual frontier. Secondly, even though no words are spoken, there is tacit acceptance of common ground by teacher and taught. The most obvious part of this is the relaxed but necessary pattern of art lessons. There is also the known and trusted skill of the teacher as an artist and, more remotely, there is the social pattern of the school and the whole field of artistic tradition in which artists work. In varying degrees John senses these as part of his environment. All he says when asked about his teacher is: 'she's not bad'. He experiments and faces unknowns in the secure knowledge that there is a framework and that he always could ask for help. He chooses among all these complications and mainly comforting pressures, to hold on to the area of freedom where he is, shaping the leopard and, unknowingly, himself. For is not even the smallest creative act reciprocal, altering the objects outside; but also altering the self?

My own interest in such situations has developed partly in ordinary or experimental teaching situations, but also in the context of mountaineering. Here one can observe a craft being learnt which produces practically nothing, yet which is indulged in with great passion. It seems to have some useful and happy effects on those, especially the young, who accept its rigours. The mountaineer is doing work very similar in training and execution to that of a craftsman, though apparently the only new 'things' that emerge are traces in his memory of skill, beauty, and struggle. Somehow these seem to enrich the performer, though how much value there is from such activity in terms of 'character training' can be left an open question. Nothing is produced, but perhaps there is a significant 'recoil' or reciprocal effect which the performer receives from his exertions.

I shall suggest a generalization which ties these two examples (the young artist and the young mountaineer) more closely and points to certain common elements. The generalization is this: that when anyone faces an area of doubt and reacts to it positively (i.e. not disregarding it or turning away), he enlarges his own field of consciousness and thereby prepares the ground for creative action. This is a statement in ordinary language of an existentialist view which unites knowledge with choice and action.

The phrase 'area of doubt' covers an extremely wide range; one might almost say that it refers to all characteristically human activity. Whenever a person's imagination is engaged, trying to project a pattern on to chaotic or conflicting experience, he is at the frontier; his own particular sector of a much greater frontier which runs through time and space. Our main concern will not be with the syntheses and insights of prophets, artists, and scientists who have perceptibly affected history but with the multitude of small achievements which include all effective education, all living ritual, all extensions of language, the play and fantasy of children, and, perhaps, the work of dreams. In later chapters we shall be much concerned with the manner in which a person faces doubt, and the images which help him to anticipate and handle it.

Our immediate question, however, is about how other people are involved.[1] How can a teacher have 'inside knowledge' of what a child is doing? Firstly, a creative initiative cannot be isolated in time and it almost always involves more than one person. Behind the young artist was a teacher and she herself is not immune from change, for 'the education of the pupil is always the self-education of the teacher'.[2] And ahead of the child will be those, friends and parents, who will be influenced by the message of his work. Despite the reciprocal relationship between teacher and pupil there is a sense in which she has authoritative knowledge about him. Anyone who has spent years acquiring a skill, gradually ascending its different levels, attains a special kind of knowledge which gives understanding of the whole process intuitively. Such intuition does not run counter to reasoned thinking but uses it. For example, a sensitive teacher will be quick to understand the kind of problem a child is facing; but will not be in a hurry to supply an answer. He will use both reason and intuition to judge the moment of intervention and also to allow for his own probable errors.

These frontier processes easily escape the net of science. Children's activity can be pinned down after a fashion, but even this is elusive. One difficulty is that the child artist intent on his picture, or the young climber at full stretch, and others in like degree of concentration, represent extremely complex wholes. You can interrupt and question them, but to do so is to break up the very activity which you wish to understand. Even if you

[1] An interesting approach to this field is being developed at Oxford by R. Harré on the basis of E. Goffman's observations. He regards the 'game model' as only adequate for the more rule-governed social interactions. Complementary models are proposed to cover freer and more creative interactions. These he terms 'dramatalurgical' and 'liturgical' models. In these, though rules still operate, *meaning* plays an increasing part. Goffman (1969) and R. Harré, unpublished paper, 'The Analysis of Episodes'.

[2] Herbert Read, *Education through Art*, p. 292.

were to rely only on careful observation, the more closely you examine your 'specimen' the more you will be likely to disturb it. This is just one of several difficulties which result from purely scientific attempts to study high-level mental activities, of which science is itself one product.[3]

On the other hand, the quiet teacher, moving about in the painting class, had a great deal of experience of this kind of situation, both as receiver and giver. Michael Polanyi in his book *Personal Knowledge*[4] has discussed in detail the knowledge which skilled people derive from 'inside' their craft—surgeons, musicians, judges, and research scientists. In his chapter on skills he distinguishes between the kind of meaning that an observer finds in analysing and comparing the components of his actions and the 'meaning which a context possesses in itself'. This he describes as '*existential*, to distinguish it from *denotative* or more generally, *representative* meaning'. He goes on to point out that the meaning of music is mainly existential, while that of a portrait may be mainly representative. The objective observer of our child artist will try to obtain precise representative meaning, enabling comparison to be made between this 'unit' and others; the sympathetic teacher on the other hand seeks mainly the other, existential understanding, trying to appreciate the whole situation of the child and to see what is potential in it.

My own standpoint in attempting to think about this frontier zone of education is that of a teacher who has sampled a good many relevant heuristic situations from within but has also had occasion to observe and reflect on them from without. The dual point of view is one which all experienced teachers develop in some measure, though for many the pressures of examinations and of over-work and, sometimes, of ambition make it hard to

---

[3] Hannah Arendt in *The Human Condition*, pp. 42–3, emphasizes the inability of statistics to reveal the most crucial acts and events, for 'the meaning and fulness of everyday relationships is disclosed not in everyday life but in rare deeds. . . . The unfortunate truth about behaviourism and the validity of its "laws" is that the more people there are, the more likely they are to behave, and the less likely they are to tolerate non-behaviour'.

[4] *Personal Knowledge*, Ch. 4.

maintain a balance. Generally the prejudices and assumptions of our society favour the objective view—all the numerical, measurable, organizational aspects of our work. But the good teacher holds this in check and cultivates the art of seeing the child subjectively or existentially, as if he or she is very marvellous and mysterious (a view that need in no way be undermined by his unflattering analysis of the same child in the staff room) and as if each child is, potentially, much greater than himself (a view that need not run counter to self-confidence, for in it lies the greatness of our vocation). It is this balance between objectivity and subjectivity, this binocular vision, that will concern us in the next chapter. But first it is necessary to examine a little further the word 'existential' and the development of thought in Europe which has made it current, a development which is related to many of our present educational frustrations and discontents.

Existentialism is usually seen as beginning with the prophetic voice of Kierkegaard as he denounces all professors who explain everything away. Darwin appeared to be explaining Nature; Hegel (and later Marx) appeared to be explaining History. Other reactions against the onward sweep of scientific explanation and technological advance took many shapes. One of these, incidentally, was mountaineering and other forms of compensatory adventure. When the upper middle class were enjoying mid-Victorian certainties and securities some—perhaps the extrovert ones—turned to the elemental doubts and hazards of mountains; others, like William Morris, turned to the rural workshop for fulfilment and escape; while Freud re-excavated the subconscious.[5] Of course these are over-simplifications, but it is possible to see here the first waves of revolt against mechanized and predetermined patterns of life. Kierkegaard made the first philosopher's protest and, though his words were little heeded at the time, his theme was taken up by others after the Second World War.

One of the difficulties of understanding existentialism is that in English the word 'existence' has a passive ring. The German

[5] Lancelot Law Whyte, *The Unconscious before Freud*, p. 13.

word *existenz* conveys an active sense, something of the be-*ing* of theology, the I AM of Jehovah, and the *esse* of essence. Existentialists are concerned with this positive quality of being and they teach that profound truths will only be known to people who are prepared to act, to choose, and to pass through that kind of experience which increases their degree of being. The concomitants of such painful choice will often be loneliness, responsibility, and anguish (*angst*).

Sartre remarks that 'man first of all exists, surges up into the world and defines himself afterwards'.[6] This has the elemental ring which one associates with existentialists, but it also indicates another important dimension. 'Man . . . defines himself afterwards.' Time comes in. The analytical mode of understanding falls into place after the action and the experience. The patterns of a language (grammar) or of a science (theory) are best experienced in action first, without analysis, and then, after a substantial amount of action and experience, comes the time for analytical discernment of the pattern. And this is true of educational theory too. Many people have remarked that the best time for teachers to appreciate educational theory is after several years of practical teaching. If you take away some of the dramatic overtones of existentialism, many of its ideas fit in with educational experience; but only, I think, if one assumes not that the explainers and analysers are of the devil, but that both the objective and subjective approaches are valid and what we need to seek is a balance between them.

The Jewish existentialist, Martin Buber, has explored this line.[7] His views on education and on creative relationships between people are very helpful. Herbert Read pays tribute to him in the closing chapters of *Education through Art,* and many people will be familiar with his distinction between mechanical *I–it* relationships (treating people like things) and the freer, mutually enhancing relationships of *I–Thou.* Such an existentialism involves other people and implies a patient struggle to move out from mechanical and predetermined situations towards

[6] Sartre, *Existentialism and Humanism*, p. 28.
[7] Martin Buber, *I and Thou* and *Between Man and Man.*

acts and experiences of freedom. Buber accepts that creative work will often involve painful choice and the anguish of trying to make a vision into a reality. The materials are often obdurate, the work may be slow, but the beginning of all new creativeness is in the communion of minds.

3 Two ways of knowing

> The 'soul' of a crystal is the form—the mathematical formula—of
> the crystal; the soul of a plant, more complex is a tendency towards
> a certain form of which time as well as space is a dimension. Soul,
> far from being a vague concept, [is], on the contrary, the principle
> of form and the formative principle which in man is imagination.
> KATHLEEN RAINE on 'The Use of the Beautiful'[1]

I must declare an assumption: that there is no division between a
spiritual and material universe, no division between mind and
body. 'The same events are known as mind from within and brain
from without.'[2] The apparent conflicts between theology and
science have always been caused by people seeing the same
phenomena from opposite directions, or because there have been,
and still are, genuine mysteries; but these mysteries are no one's
special preserve; nor do they lie inherently outside the realm of
mind and reason. Further, the nature of the encounter between
each man's 'known' and each man's 'unknown' is his most
important attribute. It is sometimes called his imagination and
this word is adequate if it covers all that he creates, his 'formative
principle' to use Kathleen Raine's term.

I cannot prove this, but would urge in its favour that it is
simpler than any dualist view; that it accepts mystery and doubt,
and that these give it a dynamic quality; and it has broad support,
being held with slight variations, by many scientists who know
what religion is about and by many religious people who know
what science is about.

A subsidiary assumption included in the above is that we see
things from two opposing directions—not just from differing
directions and that this unrecognized quality of vision has been
a main cause of schism and of dualistic world views. Two-way

[1] *Defending Ancient Springs.*
[2] In *Issues in Science and Religion* Ian Barbour surveys the territory
where science and religion overlap, with erudition and skill.

vision is fundamental to us and is related to the basic laws of physics which indicate a scale of order/disorder in the universe and which is expressed by the, now popular, second law of thermodynamics.[3] We either look down this scale to what is less organized, or up it to what is more organized. One of the novel features of the twentieth century may be that many people are bringing this inner conflict into the open and are discovering a new balance, accepting both views as complementary. Provided that we are aware of this dialectical process, there may be a further advantage in holding to a unitary world view; we are better equipped for penetrating paradox and for surviving conflict when we have a firm faith in ultimate orderliness.

Let us consider a simple example from the small-scale orderliness of matter. Here at the tip of my pencil, graphite is sliding on to the paper in a controlled avalanche, flat plate-like clusters of carbon atoms, like slatey scree. Four hooks on each atom link sideways to provide the smooth gently-adhesive quality so useful in 'lead' pencils and in lubricants. The fourness of carbon shows itself in other ways: in a lightly packed bunch to make a grain of soot or packed tightly and with three-dimensional symmetry by the intense pressure of volcanic pipes to make diamonds. These well-known transmutations of carbon, like many other underlying processes and patterns of nature, are pleasant to contemplate.

But this example of carbon is not merely an interesting

---

[3] Michael Flanders and Donald Swann give a convenient short version of this in 'At the Drop of Another Hat'. It may serve perhaps as a reminder to the reader of part of the story:

> Heat cannot of itself pass
> From one body to a hotter body;
>> Heat can't pass from a cooler to a hotter
>> You can try it if you like but you'd far better notter . . .
>
> Heat is work and work's a curse
> And all the heat in the universe can't increase
> Then there'll be no more work
> And there'll be perfect peace
>> that's entropy man.

But for the other side of the story see Schrödinger, *What is Life?* or Wiener, *Cybernetics*.

exploration down the scale of matter; it can be a starting-point for showing how our attention can move in two directions: towards what carbon is made of or towards what it could become. We can penetrate analytically 'downwards' towards electrons, through shell-like orbits and across great spaces to the atomic nucleus with its complex, still-untangled particles and untamed energy; or we can move 'up' the scale in the direction of potentiality and can reflect on the four-hooked three-dimensional pattern-building characteristics which make carbon the basic unit of living stuff. Hook the atoms together with a few oxygen and hydrogen atoms and you make sugars, the fuels of life. Add some more and you get polymers, the long chain molecules from which fibres are derived. At a much higher level of complexity, with the addition of a few other elements, the vast spiral helixes of DNA and RNA are built. These are the code-bearing molecules, each containing many million atoms whose patterns carry the encyclopedic information on which life builds up.[4]

Against whatever background order and disorder are discussed the metaphors of 'high' and 'low' are likely to creep in. It is not only in theology but also in psychology that these metaphors can trap the unwary into thinking that spatial dimensions are being referred to. I suspect that this metaphor first moved from its original context when people were thinking in terms of hierarchies in a primitive court, when literally the higher, or perhaps bigger person, held sway. At all events these words do refer to a hierarchical arrangement of concepts. Our thinking moves down towards an atomic framework from a higher molecular framework which includes the lower one; but the lower atomic frame does not of course include the molecular one. Similarly, if we move up the scale, biological conceptual frames include the molecular and atomic ones, but are not included in them. Time comes into this too. We look down the scale for causes and these are generally in the past; we look up the scale

---

[4] For a study of the 'boundary conditions' which exist between levels of inorganic, organic, and living matter and for DNA's capacity to 'evoke' rather than to 'determine' ontogenetic development see M. Polanyi's essay 'Life's irreducible structures' in *Knowing and Being*, pp. 225–39.

for larger patterns and potentialities and then our attention tends towards the future.

When we think about relatively simple things, like molecules or crystals, the mental transition, from analysing them into their constituent parts to envisaging the larger patterns which they could make, is not difficult; especially when we already know the patterns to look for. But when a discovery is actually being made, when a pattern is being perceived for the first time, then considerable imaginative powers must be deployed.[5]

It is here that symbolism plays a crucial part. This is the point we reached in the last chapter, that certain kinds of understanding require the acceptance, 'from within', of a complex mass of experience which we assume could be unified. But then we need a symbol to enable us to assimilate these diverse elements, by modifying old mental patterns or creating new ones. A symbol is an instrument for conceptual enlargement. It may sometimes be 'wrong' in that it is soon discarded, like Kepler's ingenious first model for spacing the planets,[6] or in areas of more persistent mystery it may haunt men like a myth.[7] We shall return to some of these questions later, but for the moment I will put forward a truism—that imagination works through images, and then qualify this by the less obvious distinction referred to by Polanyi, that it is not the plain representative meaning of a symbol which is important but its existential meaning, its power to change its users' thought patterns.

The power of symbols has been known to poets and prophets from the earliest times. Sometimes it has been accepted widely and used by ordinary people; often it has been perverted; often

---

[5] For a fuller treatment of this subject see T. S. Kuhn, *The Structure of Scientific Revolutions,* Chapter X.

[6] For a popular account see Koestler's *The Sleepwalkers.*

[7] I do not mean 'mere' myth in the popular sense of being untrue. 'Mythical thought always proceeds from awareness of oppositions towards their resolutions' (Levi-Strauss, *Structural Anthropology,* p. 224), and Cassirer says of myth that 'it originally grasps only the great, fundamental contrast of light and darkness and . . . treats them as one essence . . . out of which definite characters only gradually emerge' (*Language and Myth,* p. 14). Or for a deep, thoroughly unfashionable study of myth, science, and theology see E. Sewell, *The Orphic Voice.*

forgotten. Cynics say, 'these two crossed sticks are just wood' or, perhaps, 'just geometry'. Or they say, 'this myth claims to be historic fact and now we know it isn't, so it's just a story. And anyway it points to nothing new or important'. Such reductive, 'nothing but' attitudes are widespread today, but they are not new. It is interesting to hear how Origen in the third century A.D. was forced to make the sort of protest that a modern bishop might utter:

Who is so foolish to suppose that God, after the manner of a husband-man, planted a paradise in Eden towards the East and planted it with a tree of life, visible and palpable so that one tasting the fruit with bodily teeth obtained life? . . . I do not suppose that anyone doubts that these things figuratively indicate certain mysteries.[8]

But still in the twentieth century we fail to see in depth. The main function of symbolic language is not for teaching simple or childish minds. It is a method for penetrating mystery, for enlarging the mind of the wise man as well as the child. Symbols in many forms hold us with expectant doubts on the frontier of mystery. Yet this is widely neglected, as though to accept it were to embrace unreason. 'European thinkers', writes Lancelot Law Whyte, 'have tended to fall into two camps representing con-trasted tendencies in human nature; the one seeking for order and unity (often called mystical or religious) and the other [seeking] differences between particulars (the "tough" thinkers or scientists) . . . sometimes members of these two camps can scarcely speak to one another, because each stands for what the other has inhibited but uses unconsciously.'[9] It will be evident that in this territory, where many different disciplines overlap, terminology can be a problem. Law Whyte distinguishes 'mystical' from 'tough' thinkers and other pairs of terms can be used. I shall generally employ the more descriptive and less emotive terms— 'imaginative' and 'analytic'. Perceiving new patterns and possibili-ties is characteristic of the former; analysis, of the latter. But their complementary nature must always be borne in mind.

[8] Origen, *On First Principles,* iv, i. 17
[9] Law Whyte, *The Unconscious before Freud.*

Both imaginative and analytical modes of thought can be applied at all levels. A chemist searching for some new organic hypothesis[10] can contemplate a particle of matter or its relevant geometry almost as a poet would, letting his mind wander associatively round these, allowing many frames of reference to intersect and interact on each other at the focus of meditation. In contrast, a social scientist can do analytical research on prayer.[11] As we move up the scale to human and social problems, the imaginative mode becomes more and more fruitful and the analytic mode more restricted. The latter can still be usefully employed after the event, retrospectively or as some subsidiary part of a larger process.

It seems that we are slowly learning to be at home in a philosophical position which Ludwig Wittgenstein was pioneering forty years ago. In his *Philosophical Investigations* he was breaking free from his earlier view of language as having some essence of pure logic which it was his task to distil. Like the physicists of the first quarter of this century he had to escape the thrall of exactness and the hope of finding a single correct view. One or two quotations may illustrate this: '. . . Philosophy is a battle against the bewitchment of our intelligence by means of language.' 'One thinks that one is tracing the outline of a thing's nature over and over again, and one is merely tracing the frame through which one looks at it.' 'The real discovery is one that makes me capable of stopping doing philosophy when I want to.'[12]

I am not claiming support from Wittgenstein for the 'two ways of knowing' which have been sketched in this chapter. But he does seem to be saying something relevant and important when he warns us against pursuing linguistic exactness too far. Further he suggests that sometimes we are 'inside' language operating with it and that sometimes we are 'outside' language thinking about it; the poet and the grammarian. Teachers spend more time in the latter role. But there is great danger in exclusively cultivating

[10] The most famous case is von Kekulé's intuition of the hexagonal benzene ring-structure while dreaming, but there are many others.

[11] *From Cry to Word: Contributions towards a Psychology of Prayer*, ed. A. Godin.

[12] *Philosophical Investigations*, from paras. 109, 114, 133.

the pupil's taste for exactness. The good teacher must vary his approach and sometimes share the strain and darkness of genuine perplexity. Teacher and pupil must learn by joint experience that language and the conceptual framework in which it is unified *do* change and that in such transformations we ourselves change; but of this more in Chapter 5.

This is particularly relevant to problems of leadership which, almost by definition, should be concerned with situations where the rules of the game are not an adequate guide. In training people for educational administration, or business, too much emphasis is placed on decision-making. I remember a headmasters' course which was entirely built round this theme. Certainly we need to be decisive at times and coolly analytical. But the art of leadership does not lie there. It lies in the capacity which we have just been discussing—the imaginative power to discern the vague outlines of the desirable and the possible in complex human situations, outlines which must be roughly symbolized in some way so that they can be kept in mind and conveyed to others, even while they are still vague. The result may be not seeing the promised land, not thinking that an easy solution can be found, not demanding direct action but searching for deeper understanding.

We had a memorable session when Father Trevor Huddleston[13] came to talk to a sixth-form group on Sophiatown and South Africa. He found the audience well-informed about *apartheid* and equipped with the usual liberal attitudes. When, however, he saw that these were more or less prejudices, he changed gear and gave a most moving word-portrait, complete with accent and gesture, of what it felt like to be an old Boer farmer on the veld, caring for the land and the people on it and for all that his ancestors had achieved, yet troubled by all the problems and pressures of the twentieth century. The liberals among us may not have been converted but we were enriched by a little education in other men's doctrines, by feeling sympathy even when we could not agree.

This example illustrates how a symbol can become the focus

[13] Now Bishop of Stepney.

of imaginative knowing. Anyone with rudimentary knowledge and imagination can produce a mental image of a Boer farmer. But an image may not move us. What Father Huddleston did was to use this image as a focus from which to explore a complex and tragic human situation. So, for many of us, this imaginary farmer grew into a symbol, enlarging a little our own understanding of South Africa.

The conflict was untouched—good and evil deeply mixed and desperately difficult to resolve. Our teacher that night became himself something of a symbol. Through him and his imaginary antagonist we became perhaps a little less cock-sure, able to imagine those southern plains and cities and faces in more varied shades; not just in black and white.

4 Dreams and the edge of nonsense

Reason has moons, but moons not hers
Lie mirrored in her seas,
Confounding her astronomers,
But, O! delighting me.

RALPH HODGSON

On the following page is a black-and-white illustration called 'The Hidden Man'.[1] It has become quite famous. It was originally noticed by someone scanning the detail of air photographs taken by Americans flying over south-west China. It is a work of nature. If you look at it steadily, however, and without anxiety, you may come to see the vivid picture of a bearded messiah-like face, looking straight at you. The face is above and to the right of the centre point and the forehead is cut off, just above the eyes, by the top frame.

In our sixth-form course on European art we used to show this picture on the screen when discussing Gombrich's ideas[2] on the subjective, viewer's part in all seeing. In a class of about twenty-five boys, perhaps one would see the hidden man immediately. Then slowly more and more would get there. Many would need help. The two eyes or the outline of the face would be indicated. Within about ten minutes most of the class would have had the mildly exciting experience of projecting their own vivid visual schema on to this unusually effective screen. A few, with dogged honesty, would still admit to being unable to see it, even after being shown the key. If you have not already seen the face, it is worth determining to watch your own sensations as the image

[1] See also M. L. Abercrombie, *The Anatomy of Judgment*, Ch. 2. The key to this picture is printed on p. 33. But if you look at this first it will take away from the experience of 'seeing'; as explanation detracts from seeing a joke.

[2] *Art and Illusion*, especially Ch. VI, 'The Image in the Clouds'.

c

dawns, for the first impact is always the strongest, though it may take a minute or two to build up to its maximum effect.

The value of this demonstration was that it illustrated the extremely important part played in the appreciation of art by

Fig. 1a. The Hidden Man. This is the now well-known 'picture of Christ'. It is an accidental pattern of snow and rock noticed on some pre-war reconnaissance flights over the mountains of western China. Most people need time and assistance before they can *see* or project a mental schema on to this random pattern. The key has been printed on p. 33 and the reader is advised not to refer to this prematurely. If he does he will miss the mild *frisson* which may accompany the first spontaneous perception of the face.

Here are some clues: the face occupies the top half of the plate, just to the right of the middle line. The top margin cuts across just above the eyebrows. The main mass of black in the top half is either shaggy hair and beard or shadow outlining and high-lighting the face. The circular white dot is a high-light in the shadowed left-hand eye (his right). When the image starts to form watch your own reactions and, later, other people's.

our individual power to project imaginative schemata on to any picture that we see, a power which varies both with the individual and with the picture. It is obvious of course that nothing is thrown out by the eye or mind—unless one were to speak in some 'spiritual' sense. The word 'project' is a metaphor referring to the workings of certain mental frames or *gestalt*. A pattern of relative disorder (rock and snow) comes—in this case by chance

—to fit into a more complex pattern or process which might be called 'face recognition'.

In his *Art and Illusion*[3] E. H. Gombrich shows how many painters who tried to explain their techniques relied partly on such disorderly patterns to 'quicken the spirit of invention'. Leonardo da Vinci, for example, gives the following advice:

> You should look at certain walls stained with damp, or at stones of uneven colour. If you have to invent some backgrounds you will be able to see in these the likeness of divine landscapes . . .; and then again you will see there battles and strange figures in violent action.

Many children see faces in clouds and pictures in the foliage of trees. So did Shakespeare. Yet it is a process in which teachers and psychologists seem only to have a small interest. The Rorschach ink-blot tests have proved their value in assessing personality, and of course many art teachers exploit such methods. When we did our 'hidden man' experiment at Abbotsholme it was interesting to watch the strange buzz of excitement which this achievement of insight produced. I could not help wondering what was the nature of the process we were involved in and why it was that such experiences should be rare in school and in the life of an adolescent.

This chapter and the two which follow are about three important but somewhat obscure areas of experience which all touch the frontier where patterns emerge from apparent chaos. These areas are: *dreams and nonsense, words and symbols,* and *skilled action.* I shall discuss quite briefly some of the recent views of psychologists who seem to offer a helpful approach to these phenomena. Then in each chapter I shall put forward tentatively an idea of my own which may extend our understanding of these and of their possible relationship to each other.

DREAMS FROM THE OUTSIDE

The last ten years has seen a great advance in our understanding of sleep and the beginnings of a scientific theory of

[3] p. 188.

dreaming. But still no one has any idea of why we do these things. The work of people like Kleitman in Chicago and Oswald[4] in Edinburgh has made it clear that there are two quite distinct kinds of sleep. This research has been largely based on the electroencephalograph (e.e.g.), which records accurately the slight changes in electrical activity of the brain. One rhythm of discharge, quite different from the normal waking rhythm, goes on during orthodox sleep. The other rhythm corresponds to regular but shorter periods of what is called paradoxical sleep. During the latter most of the larger muscles of the body are in a state of extreme relaxation, but the eyes, under their closed lids, move about rapidly and the brain appears to be very active. Even people who say they do not dream will recall vivid dreams if woken up during periods of paradoxical sleep and asked to relate them. The so-called non-dreamers are people who never or rarely wake up during paradoxical sleep. Paradoxical sleep takes place for about ten minutes in every ninety minutes of orthodox sleep.

Orthodox sleep is not entirely free from dream-like activity. Many people see what are called hypnagogic images during the early stages of orthodox sleep. These are often abstract or surrealist pictures, but they lack the chronological and dramatic character of true dreams. Sleep-talking is more common in orthodox sleep, and sleep-walking never takes place in the other, paradoxical periods.

Both kinds of sleep are essential. Experiments have been carried out in which volunteers are deprived of paradoxical sleep. Whenever the electroencephalogram showed that they were approaching the paradoxical period, the volunteers were woken up. As the process continued, over several nights, they would start the first paradoxical rhythms more and more early, as though they were trying to make up what they had lost. During the day these volunteers would get increasingly irritable till, eventually, they were allowed to sleep uninterruptedly. Then they would indulge in considerably more paradoxical sleep than

---

[4] See N. Kleitman, 'Patterns of Dreaming', *Scientific American*, November 1960; Edwin Diamond, *The Science of Dreams*; Ian Oswald, *Sleep*.

before, though they did not need to make up the full amount which they had lost.

This is a very brief summary of extremely interesting and ingenious work which has been done in this field. In his book *Sleep* Ian Oswald makes entertaining criticism of psychotherapists, especially the Freudians, who take the hidden meaning of dreams seriously. Yet doubt persists. Though the psychoanalysts have possibly merited some antagonism, may it not be that there is sometimes an important kind of sense to be fished out from this personal pool of dreaming non-sense?

DREAMS FROM INSIDE

I write with the enthusiasm and therefore the bias of someone who has much enjoyed occasional bouts of dreaming. Undoubtedly some dreams are very unpleasant and seem to be thrusting a morsel of hell and corruption on one's attention. Jung would say that these represent something from my dark 'shadow' side, a compensation for my normal pose of respectability. This sounds at least plausible. But other dreams are sublime. Both extremes, duly salted with reason, can point to unexpected conclusions which experience proves apt.

The ideas about the meaning of dreams which I have found most helpful come from Jung. There are of course other respectable theories, and undoubtedly some of Jung's writings need viewing with scepticism. He accepted the basic findings of Freud, but diverged and eventually quarrelled with him on the kind of explanation that could be offered for dreams and other odd mental occurrences. Freud, especially in his earlier phases, maintained that explanations of dreams must relate to the past experience of any particular individual. Jung accepted the importance of childhood experience but suggested that we should sometimes seek explanations in the 'experience' of the whole human race and in its genetically transmitted tendencies and patterns. Jung also showed more interest in the future. The meaning of a dream was to be understood in terms of what might happen as well as what had happened.

Both men would probably have agreed that dreams are often a symbolical representation of some stress which the conscious mind cannot yet accept, and that understanding the symbols of a dream resolves tension and may introduce new truth to the mind of the dreamer. But Jung took a wider view of the unconscious than Freud and regarded it as more than the repository of suppressed wishes and memories. He agreed that it performs these functions, but added that it also displays patterns inherited biologically, just as we inherit the basic patterns of our bodies. These brain-patterns and the effects which they produce through the unconscious mind he called *archetypes*.

In his essay 'On Psychical Energy' Jung shows that he is aware of the danger that he will be accused of postulating inherited ideas. He writes: 'What is meant is rather, inherited possibilities of ideas.' And later:

Although our inheritance consists in physiological paths, still it was mental processes in our ancestors which created these paths. If these traces come to consciousness again in the individual, they can do so only in the form of mental processes; and if these processes . . . appear as individual acquisitions, they are none the less pre-existing traces, which are merely 'filled out' by the individual experience. Every 'impressive' experience is such an impression, in an ancient but previously unconscious stream bed.[5]

There are several phrases in this passage which help to clear the way for a deeper understanding of symbolism. Jung is first outlining his theory of archetypes, secondly he is emphasizing the unmetaphysical (monist) nature of his theory, and thirdly he is introducing a slightly complex idea about mental events 'filling out' cerebral pathways. Let us consider these in order.

The archetype hypothesis was postulated by Jung when he recognized in his patients' dreams certain symbols which he believed could not have entered through their senses and conscious apprehension. He did not postulate any form of thought transference across time and space, but suggested that inherited, common patterns in the brain have an effect on the activities of

[5] *Contributions to Analytical Psychology*, p. 60.

the mind, just as inherited common patterns in our bodies—the form of the hand for instance—affect the things we make and do. Jung assumed that these archetypal patterns are imprinted on the evolving human stock through millions of years of human and sub-human evolution. He recognized in mythology and in many artistic and religious phenomena man's attempt to express and come to terms with these patterned, shaping forces which are effective in the unconscious.[6]

Jung named and described many of the more conspicuous archetypes, though here again he is cautious, referring to them sometimes as 'constellations', with the implication, I think, that as with celestial constellations, both see-er and the stars contribute to the naming process. The *anima* is the name he gives to the female pattern, latent in the male. The *animus* is the converse form. In the northern Sudan I came across a manifestation of this in gatherings of partially urbanized women who sometimes used a form of group therapy for helping a neurotic. The ritual was called *Zar* and it involved fancy dress, acting, and rhythmic dancing. It is not uncommon for the afflicted female to dress up as some notorious male, Lord Kitchener for example. One assumes that this, in some way, helped her to come to terms with the hidden *animus* within. Wonderful are the gifts of imperialism!

This is one example of an archetype which finds symbolic expression in the personal guise of dream actors, but others are more general and non-personal, like recurring dramatic scenery. The edge of the sea is one such image and this is interesting

[6] Here we touch on a notion with important applications elsewhere: the idea that an information pattern (genetically or culturally transmitted, and note that such transmission is usually linear—DNA, discursive speech, or print) may yield different embodiments or 'meanings' according to the circumstances in which the information becomes active. A few of the contrasting areas of thought where such 'double determinedness' is being examined are mentioned on p. 96. The phrase 'double determined' is from R. O. Kapp. It is double because we must understand such complex causation to be the result both of relatively simple and specifiable past causes and of a total field of present influences which may be unspecifiable (see chapter on skills) or only partly specifiable. This is exceptionally interesting and tricky territory.

because it illustrates the difference between Freud's and Jung's understanding of what dream symbols mean. Freud was the first to recognize the significance of many of these symbols, but in general he proposed retrospective meanings. Dreams of the sea pointed back to the womb, to the amniotic fluid in which the foetus lay. A Jungian would look both forward and back, saying something like this: 'Yes, the dream of a dive into the sea may well have roots in embryonic experience but it goes beyond that. The experiences of passing through, and under, water has left traces on the evolving brains of humans and even far back into the animal world. Its origin is archetypal; but its full meaning— ah!—that is still with us and in the future. What do you think? It was your dream.'[7]

The second thing to notice about Jung's attitude to the meaning of dreams is that he is more wary than is sometimes assumed of coming to religious and transcendental conclusions. He stresses that 'every statement about the transcendental ought to be avoided because it is a laughable presumption on the part of the human mind, unconscious of its limitations. Therefore when God or *Tao* is spoken of as a stirring of, or condition of the soul, something has been said about the knowable only, but nothing about the unknowable'.[8] In these quotations Jung is backing away from anything that might imply the dualist view of nature that his opponents would like to attack.

Even though dream theory is rudimentary, and even though psychoanalysis may sometimes have caused the meaning of dreams to be exaggeratedly or falsely construed, they may still be very important in their relationship to imagination. The life of many people in modern society is dangerously dull and extrovert. Why are we not bolder about using our unconscious sources as a normal practice? Why should not children and healthy adults be taught about dreams? These doors of perception are

---

[7] A friendly critic, Margaret Hodgson, who knows far more about Freud than I, says that in fact Freud and most psychoanalysts are a good deal less retrospective than I suggest.

[8] From Jung's commentary on Wilhelm's translation of *The Secret of the Golden Flower*. Jung's explanation of the meaning of *Tao*, the way of wisdom which reconciles psychological opposites, is extremely helpful.

part of us. They need not be shut and require no poisonous kicks to force them open. Even with dreams of course there are some dangers. People can get their priorities wrong and allow fantasies to take precedence over reason. No matter how impressive the inward journey seems, the duller, outward life is always what it refers to, always the place, either through work or waiting, where reality must be faced. In a strange way too the timing of dreams can be relied on. If you miss an image today, it will probably come again. This quality of dreams is one of the things which makes me mistrust violent, hypnotic or chemical means for procuring them. With Jonathan Miller, 'I resent the idea of being raped into the Higher Sensitivity.'[9]

A CONFLICT AND A HYPOTHESIS

Experimental psychologists like Oswald or Eysenck often express impatience with the pronouncements of psychoanalysts. The following criticism is characteristic and contains some extremely interesting ideas which Oswald does not develop.

It is easy to understand why analysts of differing theoretical persuasions can each quote dreams to illustrate the truth of what each personally believes. Each does it by discussing an unrepresentative cross-section. Furthermore, experimental psychologists can show us how sadly unreliable memory is, and how, if a thing is only dimly remembered, we manufacture what seems appropriate at the time of recall, doing so in all honesty and unaware of our own invention. What patients describe to their analysts are probably partly *day-time fantasies, to some degree fashioned (all unawares)* to please the analyst. *These fantasies may usefully illustrate the patient's personality structure* but cannot be reliable evidence of what went on by night.

. . . The astrologers of ancient civilizations foretold the future from both dreams and stars. In the course of their work and in the midst of several erroneous theories about the solar system they achieved remarkable knowledge and extraordinary skill in predicting the movements of the various heavenly bodies.[10]

---

[9] Article on drugs in *Vogue*, September 1967.
[10] *Sleep*, p. 84, my italics.

It should be pointed out that the analysts are not much interested in 'what went on during the night'; that is much more Oswald's field; they are interested in the vivid stories the patients tell them. In a similar way, though with less confidence, one might suggest that ancient astrologers only partly shared modern scientists' interest in accurate prediction. Like the psychoanalyst, they may have been more concerned with mental health and with their clients' ability to cope with next week's problems.

In the passages I have italicized Oswald seems to be on the verge of making an important suggestion; but he does not develop it, partly perhaps because it would mean conceding more to the psychiatrists than he would like. Why should we not accept his suggestion that 'partly day-time fantasies' are what the patient and therapist are interested in? Why not follow this up and consider the possibility that being woken from paradoxical sleep presents someone with a highly personal chunk of dis-order on which he can project pictures of great significance? This puts Leonardo's damp walls, the astrologer's star chaos, the chiaroscuro of snow and rock on p. 22, and my fleeting experience of paradoxical sleep in the same category. But with one important distinction: that when I drowsily experience the fading activity of paradoxical sleep it is part of 'me', not plaster or stars or snow patterns. The image is seen, not on the screen, but in the mind of the beholder.

This raises difficulties, but so does the current divergent state of dream theory. It has been found for example that cats have very active paradoxical sleep periods and rapid eye movement. Most higher vertebrates appear to share this, though in varying degrees. Are we to suppose that when a cat is having paradoxical sleep it is also enjoying a rich visual scene to which its eye-movements bear testimony? If so we are making a big assumption about cats' powers of eidetic or visual recall. (For the sake of simplicity I am speaking only of visual images and leaving out sensory and auditory recall.) There is evidence that young children attain such eidetic powers at a relatively late stage—about $1\frac{1}{2}$ years of age. Cats and other vertebrates have excellent powers of memory and recognition; but this is very different from the complex additional ability which humans have of recalling a total picture—with full sound and colour.

We can get past this difficulty if we make a distinction between a physiological activity in the sleeping body of humans or vertebrates, which affects especially the eye and brain, and the mental processes which occur when the human organism rises above a certain level of activity. This 'consciousness' can apparently operate, fleetingly, on the threshold between paradoxical sleeping and waking, and when it does we call it 'remembering a dream'. It could also be called 'having' or 'projecting' a dream.

Here is a model which may help to illustrate the concept which I am suggesting. There is an enormously efficient and well-stocked library, almost entirely mechanized. There is in it one active director who co-ordinates the main research projects of the library. During the day the director, using many complex devices, refers to and puts on the tables millions of references from a great number and variety of sources—some even come from antiquity (in reprints and translations, of course, not in their originals). When darkness comes the director goes down to a basement and sleeps. During the night it becomes necessary for all the reference books and cards to be re-sorted and re-shelved. This happens in bursts of automated activity. Most of the references go back to old places, some are re-classified and new references are added, a mechanical process which does not depend on the director, except in so far as he has introduced the new references. Occasionally at night the director wakes and walks briefly out into the halls and corridors. Sometimes all is quiet and the lights are off; but occasionally he comes across great activity. Here he sometimes sees familiar references being passed to and fro. Unfamiliar ones are also thrown out in the re-sorting. Strange juxtapositions appear. From these bizarre experiences he occasionally assembles odd literary creations which he may write down and remember, or may forget. Sometimes in his routine work of the day these odd memories from the edge of sleep give him unexpected ideas which influence the normally conventional course he steers. Sometimes his encounters

with paradox even suggest new ways of organizing his own procedures and the library itself.

'The Director' is a cheat without whom there could be no
model. By simplifying the brain to the level of a library, I elimi-
nated the possibility of that high-level activity of organic tissue,
which we call consciousness, and this had to be re-introduced in
the form of a ghost in the machine.

One difficulty about this idea is that the first recall of a dream
feels very much like the memory of something past. Yet what else
could it feel like when there is no screen visible on to which we
are projecting? The disorderly references that confront us are
part of us and from our past. If you watch your first recall of a
fading dream carefully you will usually find that the story comes
to you chronologically backwards. On second recall and during
your boring re-telling of it at breakfast it will usually follow a
conventional chronology. You may also observe that sometimes
a dream follows a branching pattern. This explains many alleged
time anomalies. One key symbol can act as 'points' from which
more than one associative line of images can be followed. There
is no 'before' and 'after' in these branch lines; it is only when
one re-tells the dream that the diverging bits have to be fitted
into a linear story. The real starting-point of a dream is the
particular reference that was active in the paradoxical shuffling
of the brain at the moment of waking. From that moment on, provided you remain on the threshold of sleep, you can link other
lively references and dress them in whatever finery is lying about.
What about all the periods of paradoxical sleep when no dreams
were snatched by consciousness? Physiological equilibrium will
have been re-established, the information banks will have been
cleared and re-stored—we do not yet know what this information
sorting process involves, but it is obviously essential if the
highly developed vertebrate brain is to avoid becoming over-
programmed. 'Remembered dreams' can now be seen as symbolic
bonus gained after the routine operations have been completed.

It may be that this hypothesis creates more problems than it
solves. But it has the advantage of reducing the gap between
those who see dreams as significant and theraputic and those

who see them as noise and nonsense. Like the picture of 'The Hidden Man' the bare information may contain little 'sense' but this nevertheless can claim a high-level imaginative response from us. At the level of brain the paradoxical stirrings can be seen as useful 'noise'—meaningless because unconscious, but even so not information-less. At the level of mind the same stirrings may be the raw material for a work of image building. The same atoms are busy, but at different levels of orderliness and therefore at different levels of meaning.

FIG. 1b. Key to 'The Hidden Man'.
(Both pictures from P. B. Porter in the *American Journal of Psychology*, vol. 67, p. 550.)

5 Signs and symbols

When the process of concept formation is seen in all its complexity, it appears as a *movement* of thought within the pyramid of concepts, constantly alternating between two directions, from the particular to the general and from the general to the particular.
VYGOTSKY, *Thought and Language*

We have all of us experienced one period of intense, creative mental enlargement when, as infants, our conceptual world first took shape. This frontier is almost entirely hidden from memory, though the influence of those momentous months is always with us. Then language was born for each of us.

There are interesting similarities between the fleeting moments of 'dream memory', as described in the last chapter, and the forgotten birth of words in infancy. Both happen at a dawning of human consciousness, both probably involve a great activity of mental images, and both are an attempt by the mind to project order on to apparent disorder. There are also resemblances between these and the obscure first dawning of consciousness in *homo sapiens*. For children, and perhaps for early man, the chief thing that is made at these creative thresholds is a special kind of noise, words.

One witness who has important evidence to give about the threshold of childhood is Helen Keller, who was deaf and blind from infancy. The often-quoted passage from her autobiography, below, makes a good introduction to the fundamental relationship between words (written or spoken) and concepts, those inward activities to which words refer. Helen Keller's experience had a vivid and perhaps unique quality. This was partly because she was an unusually intelligent and sensitive person. She also happened to be born when people were beginning to take more interest in this kind of problem. Braille had just been perfected. Yet she lived through all her early childhood without any

successful education. Had she been born today her story would
have been less dramatic, for she would have been taught by special
methods from an early age. She was seven years old when the
moment of illumination came. For a few weeks she had been
receiving help from a devoted teacher who had been trying to
impress on her that m-u-g, spelt out on her hand, was mug and
that w-a-t-e-r was the stuff that can be poured or drunk. But she
persisted in confusing the two. Then she recalls the great moment:

Miss Sullivan . . . brought me my hat and I knew I was going out into
the warm sunshine. This thought, if a wordless sensation may be
called a thought, made me hop and skip with pleasure.

We walked down the path to the well-house, attracted by the
fragrance of the honeysuckle with which it was covered. Someone
was drawing water and my teacher placed my hand under the spout.
As the cool stream gushed over one hand she spelled into the other
the word *water*, first slowly, then rapidly. I stood still, my whole
attention fixed upon the motions of her fingers. Suddenly I felt a
misty consciousness as of something forgotten—a thrill of returning
thought; and somehow the mystery of a language was revealed to me.
I knew then that 'w-a-t-e-r' meant that wonderful cool something
that was flowing over my hand. That living word awakened my soul,
gave it light, hope, joy, set it free! There were barriers still, it is true,
but barriers which could in time be swept away.

I left the well-house eager to learn. Everything had a name and
each name gave birth to a new thought. As we returned to the house
every object which I touched seemed to quiver with life.[1]

Since then psychology and philosophy have begun to clarify
the complex nature of the process in which words and concepts
operate. The ideas presented here have been developed partly
by philosophers such as Ernst Cassirer and Susanne Langer,[2] but
also by psychologists like J. Piaget and L. S. Vygotsky, who have
evolved helpful experimental techniques for studying the detailed
stages of conceptual development. Nevertheless our ignorance in

[1] *The Story of My Life,* pp. 23 and 24. The passage is also quoted by
Arthur Koestler in *The Act of Creation* and by Susanne Langer in
Philosophy in a New Key.
[2] See especially Cassirer, *An Essay on Man*; Vygotsky, *Thought and
Language*; and Langer, *Philosophy in a New Key* and *Philosophical
Sketches.*

this field is great, especially in the frontier zone towards which our probings point. In this chapter we shall explore the meanings of several essential terms which relate to the interlocking relationship of words and concepts. The following terms will be examined in some detail, and it will be seen that they fit together in a hierarchical relationship. Firstly we will consider 'signal', which is a sub-mental communicating device; secondly 'concept', which is relevant to words at all levels; thirdly 'sign', which includes most words in their ordinary concept-linked use; fourthly 'symbol', which includes words and other signs when they operate dynamically, changing the people who use them, and sometimes changing their own field of reference in the process; finally we shall consider 'sacrament', whose meaning is best understood through its action in a community. We shall also have to take a wary look at 'meaning', a famous problem word.

At this threshold of speech there is a large area of uncertainty which we must hurry by. Nevertheless some of the most intractable problems should at least be indicated:

(*a*) How and to what degree did the evolutionary process accelerate during the few million years which saw the development of speech and conceptual thought in *homo sapiens* as he emerged from his pre-human ancestors?

(*b*) To what extent is this process recapitulated in the development of a child?

(*c*) The whole problem of competence: in what does cerebral and vocal competence for speech consist? What pre-human evolutionary factors favoured the emergence of these elements before the threshold of conceptual thought was reached? After it was reached it is not difficult to imagine the host of new possibilities which would become subject to accelerated development and selection, though here too lie innumerable problems.

I mention these questions only to stress that, as yet, we do not know the answers. It is a field on which many lines of inquiry are already converging, and it is of extreme interest to teachers. Some of the issues discussed in this book touch on these problems, and our approach will therefore be tentative and speculative. First, however, we must draw some distinctions in terminology. The reader should be warned that though the definitions which I suggest are in accord with some authorities, there are others who would not accept them. Some writers confuse terms—signal, sign, symbol, for example—through not understanding the difference or through not accepting the differing levels at which language operates.

A signal is a device for spreading an item of information widely with relatively small expenditure of energy. It is something that a sensitive machine can be made to obey. All animals show in greater or lesser degree the ability to adjust their actions to signals from outside. Our senses are specialized mechanisms for reacting to faint and distant signals, and they help to keep us more or less in equilibrium with a very complicated environment. Most training of animals is done by using signals and suitable rewards and punishments. One could, for example, train a dog to react in a certain way when it saw a triangle. Or one could go further and train it to respond to a more complex shape, to run its eye along a line of letters till it reached, say, the letter C. If it then barked it might have earned its biscuit, but it would not have taken the first step in learning to read. It responded to 'C' as a signal but not as a sign which carries extra information and links it in some obscure way with special potentialities in the brain.

There is a great literature of learning theory derived from the work of Pavlov and his followers. Our resulting understanding of conditioned reflexes and of stimulus-response (or signal-response) behaviour in animals and children is undoubtedly of value.[3] Nevertheless, too few writers on learning theory emphasize the extent to which humans operate in ways which are qualitatively different from those of animals. The great contribution of men like Piaget, Vygotsky, and Bruner has been, not merely to show the magnitude of the gap which separates child thinking from animal thinking, but to forge experimental probes for exploring it.

At present it is probably safest to assume that the gap is very

[3] *Learning, an Introduction* by Kathleen O'Connor gives a useful outline.

great, but not absolute. Experiments with higher apes, porpoises, and even with some birds suggest that they may be on the threshold of conceptual thought. But in general we may assume that the ability to use concepts and the signs that go with them is the essential characteristic of humans and must be studied mainly in human situations.

An experiment with chimpanzees showed the disadvantage they suffer from not being able to form concepts; and it also indicates what a concept is.[4] Two chimpanzees were provided with a platform on which was placed a food box, open on one side. Along this side was a row of small burning wicks which prevented the chimpanzees from getting the food. Nearby was a tap and a cup. The chimpanzees discovered, after trying many experiments, that the tap water could be used for extinguishing the flame. Later the tap was removed to another platform and the whole yard surrounding both platforms was flooded with water. Planks were provided so that the chimpanzees could build a bridge and this the chimpanzees succeeded in doing. They crossed the bridge, *filled the cup at the tap*, and came back to secure the food. Doubtless in time they might discover that the 'stuff in the moat' was as good a fire extinguisher as the 'stuff in the tap'. But they could not conceptualize water, as Helen Keller did, holding an image of its essence in her mind.

Concept and Sign. No one yet knows what a concept is in terms of brain circuitry or coding. Even the nature of animal memory still eludes scientific inquiry. It is impossible to locate an actual place in the brain where memories are stored. It is as though they were stored in dispersed fashion, like folklore in a tribe. Another analogy which is being followed up is that memory may be stored in a manner similar to refraction patterns, the kind of shimmering image which is thrown up by the interaction of two or more patterned screens;[5] again the information is diffused

---

[4] J. Bronowski, *Insight*, pp. 96–7.
[5] Karl H. Pribram, 'The Neurophysiology of Remembering', *The Scientific American*, vol. 220, no. 1 (Jan. 1969), 73, and A. R. Luria, 'The Functional Organization of the Brain', ibid., vol. 222, no. 3 (March 1970).

throughout, and destruction of large parts of the system do not destroy the image. When 'ordinary' animal memory is so complex in its material groundwork, we may assume that it will be a long time before there is scientific knowledge about the mechanisms

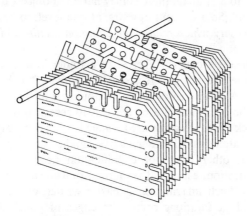

FIG. 2. One of the simplest record systems which incorporates both a cumulative record and a mechanism for selective 'abstraction' is the punched-card system. Each line of holes represents a binary option— 'yes' (closed hole) or 'no' (open hole). One or more rods can be used for withdrawing cards with particular sets of shared characteristics.

of the more abstruse and specifically human system of concepts. However, though its physiological nature remains obscure, we do know something about its psychological functioning. The concept system bears an interesting and somewhat complex relationship to objects outside the brain and to the signs—also outside the brain—which represent it. Consider the word 'carbon' as an example of a sign. As printer's ink is made partly of carbon we might regard the material of this smudge

as being the thing, or as one of the great class of things, which 'carbon' stands for.

As a result of our experience in childhood of burnt matches, soot, and coal, we have built up a generalized picture of carbon.

It is very unlikely that we could have done this without language. Later we learnt elementary chemistry and extended the framework to include graphite and diamond. The newly acquired scientific schema of atomic and molecular relationships enabled us to assimilate these somewhat alien objects to the concept 'carbon'. So a concept appears, at one level, to be *a pattern of brain activity which relates the common qualities of different things.*[6]

I have heard a concept likened to a folder in a filing cabinet where all the relevant papers are held together. But this is much too simple. A closer analogy, though doubtless also far too crude, might be the operation of a punched-card record system (Fig. 2). Here a stack of record cards are arranged in a basic—say chronological or alphabetical order. They might represent a firm's clients. But other forms of classification need to be rapidly applied—location, estimated resources, or known preferences of each client. Such information is easily written on the card but a system of perforations round the edges of punched-open or punched-closed holes permits an operator to pass a rod through all the cards and hook out only the closed perforations. He could, for example, quickly abstract details of all customers with estimated incomes of over £5,000. He can look at them without removing them from the basic order. There are of course much more sophisticated developments of this principle in computer memory stores. But what may be common between these and mental conceptual recall is that one store of records is accessible to a great variety of selective patterns. The operation of 'selective patterns' is the key idea here, and it is one which underlies a good deal of the argument of this book. I cite this simple mechanical example for those who, like myself, cannot follow all the advances of brain physiology and communications theory yet are interested in the emergence of ideas which mutually illuminate our various disciplines.

[6] Marjorie Grene, writing of the mind's activity rather than of the brain's patterns, defines concepts as 'rules for the ordering of experience' (*The Knower and the Known,* p. 142). These 'rules' are usually unconscious, part of what she and Polanyi would call 'tacit knowledge'.

We have not come very far by saying that a concept is a particular kind of selective process in the brain. We could go further and speak of mental processes. Conceptualization would now be regarded as the process of recognizing the class to which something may belong. When we do this we name the thing or the experience; we give it a sign. It will now be seen that 'sign' and 'concept' are closely related, but they are distinct. The relationship between them and the terms used to describe the processes in which they operate is summarized in the diagram (Fig. 3).

We are now in a position to attempt the definition of a sign: it is *a specialized kind of signal which works by activating concepts* . . . This definition could be finished off with the phrase 'in the brain' or 'in the mind', according to whether we were speaking in physiological or psychological terms. But the fact that 'concept' can be used without great strain in either context emphasizes the fact that it stands for a highly speculative and still mysterious kind of brain activity.

As you read the letters c–a–r–b–o–n a process should occur— the activation of the concept pattern in your brain which covers charcoal, graphite, etc.—all carbon you have known and all you might know. This process is known as connotation. Because a concept refers to what might be as well as to what has been, we are probably right to regard a concept as giving its user some degree of open, even questioning, alertness. It represents a special competence or preparedness as well as a system of records. If, when the concept 'carbon' is at the ready, you see a piece of black stuff on the paper and identify it, name it as being referred to by this concept, a threefold process is complete: name (or sign)— concept—black stuff. This linking of conceptual pattern to specific object is called *denotation*. One can contrast this more complex circuit with the simpler operation of a signal. If a piece of black coal flies at your eye and you blink without forming any concept of what is happening, the coal is then only a signal to a much simpler reflex nerve action.

The double relationship of the mental concept to both a sign and to an external class of things helps to clarify the double meaning of the word 'meaning'. This can be either connotation

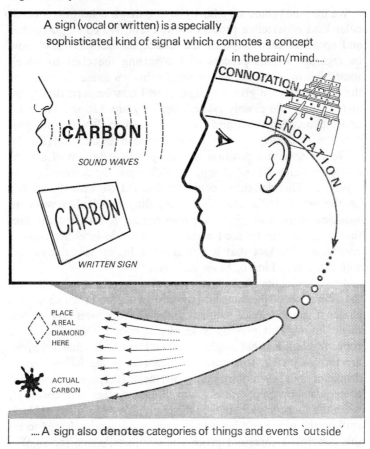

A sign (vocal or written) is a specially sophisticated kind of signal which connotes a concept in the brain/mind....

CONNOTATION

DENOTATION

CARBON

SOUND WAVES

CARBON

WRITTEN SIGN

PLACE A REAL DIAMOND HERE

ACTUAL CARBON

.... A sign also **denotes** categories of things and events `outside´

FIG. 3. The process of *signification* which involves the operation of a sign. The sign used here is the word 'carbon', either spoken or written. Its signification is dual, since it *denotes* certain classes of referent 'outside the mind' and *connotes* a concept in the mind. The punched-card arrangement within the head is a symbol for something science has not yet discovered, namely the physical pattern of cerebral activity underlying the mental process which we recognize as conceptualizing.

The three main divisions in the diagram represent the media of communications, the activity of the brain and sense organs, and, at the bottom, the field of present and potential experience.

or denotation. We can say: 'This word "carbon" means (connotes) my internal concept—my general capacity for handling that class of thing'; or we can say: 'It means (denotes) this black stuff and other possible external examples of its class.' True language is built mainly of signs, but these always work by activating concepts. They include oral words, written words, many mathematical signs, and some others. A Union Jack is a kind of sign. It may connote the big emotive mental concept, My Country, but it also denotes this real bit of ground about me and the other bits of the Kingdom which I know or might know. Connotation points to an internal process; denotation points to an external field.

Symbols. A distinction must be drawn between symbol and sign, though these sometimes merge. I shall follow Jung and Susanne Langer in regarding symbols as a special class of sign whose function is not only communication but also, and essentially transformation.[7] Jung writes: 'The psychological machine which transforms energy is the symbol. I mean a real symbol and not a sign.'[8] He does not negotiate the difficulties raised by his reference to energy very successfully, but his main distinction is clear. Susanne Langer makes the same point with somewhat more caution. She maintains that the definition of a symbol must be based on its 'formulative function' and then she offers her definition as: 'Any device whereby we make an abstraction.'[9] I think she ought to stress that 'make' here means 'create'. If her 'make' merely means 'use' then this definition might serve for all signs. Elsewhere[10] she indicates quite clearly that she regards symbols in the former sense. In the distinction between sign and

[7] *Contributions to Analytical Psychology*, Ch. I, 'On Psychical Energy'.

[8] A useful discussion of this full meaning of 'symbol' and of its etymology will be found in 'What is a Symbol supposed to be?' by Leopold Stein, *Journal of Analytical Psychology*, vol. ii, no. 1 (Jan. 1957). I am grateful to Dr. Camilla Bosanquet for this.

[9] *Philosophical Sketches*, p. 63.

[10] *Philosophy in a New Key*. In her preface to the 1951 edition Susanne Langer clears up earlier confusion between signs and signals. But there still remains here and in *Philosophical Sketches* a slight lack of distinction between sign and symbol.

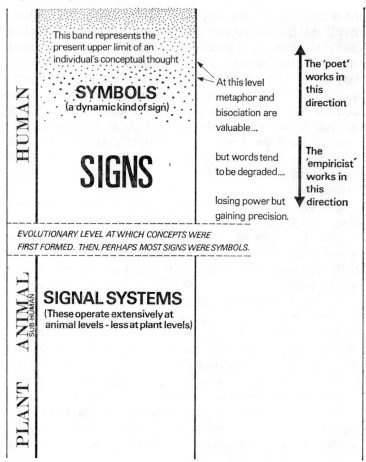

FIG. 4. This diagram suggests the relationship between three communication levels. Signs are specially sophisticated signal which always relate to concepts. Symbols are often treated as being equivalent to signs; but they should be distinguished as a special kind of sign, playing a part in the creation and enlargement of concepts. A weakness in the diagram is that it tries to show both the creative frontier of an individual (top stippled band) and the evolutionary threshold of *homo sapiens*. The reader who is interested might care to consider whether this difficulty could have been overcome.

symbol we are dealing with a gradual shift of function. I have summarized these and related ideas in the diagram (Fig. 4).[11]

It will now be evident that, at one extreme of signs, a scientist who is communicating objective facts and relationships will try to keep all emotive and symbolic meanings out of his discourse; at the other extreme, a poet will use skill and imagination to push his language 'up' the scale so that his own concepts and those of his readers' are changed by his words. There are, of course, intermediate categories. The writer of advertising copy, for example, may try to use the poet's symbols, but without his subjectivity, without the total commitment of the poet to his words. His personal position in regard to the frontier of existential commitment can be curiously anomalous.

We can recognize in language a two-way polarity, which corresponds to the two main ways in which we extend our knowledge—the ways of analysis and of imagination. We notice a further correspondence between these and the two directions of the processes of nature (towards more and towards less disorder). The implications of all this are far-reaching and beyond the scope of this book. Nevertheless, whenever in practice we approach our own or the world's most serious problems, we will find ourselves moving away from the objective, analytical stance into an existential one, in which concepts are less stable and where symbolic processes operate on ourselves and on our neighbours. Symbols cannot remain private 'mind enlargers'; they ultimately become part of language and of the culture in which we all live and change. Marshall McLuhan points out that 'our need today is

[11] The important distinction between sign and symbol is often overlooked. Glenn Langford in his *Philosophy and Education* demotes both terms. He describes (pp. 38 and 39) rats responding to *signs* (where we should say 'signals') and a jar of herbs labelled with the symbol 'rosemary' (where we should say 'sign'). This is not the place to speculate on possible reasons for the fashionable tendency to ignore the higher symbolic reaches of language. But we should beware; for a false simplicity is thus often introduced into a complex situation. What will be the effect on a future teacher of English literature if he thinks that symbolism is no more than naming or labelling? 'There's rosemary, that's for remembrance; pray, love, remember'—are Ophelia's words meant to be just botanical identification?

culturally the same as the scientist's who seeks to become aware of the bias of his instruments'.[12] But, unlike the 'pure' scientist, neither McLuhan nor you nor I can escape from our new emergent 'global village'. Are we waiting for, seeking for, new symbolic forms to give it coherence, to provide the feelings as well as the theories of brotherhood?[13] Or are the images already here, awaiting our response? These are deep questions, but they are certainly not remote from the world's travail.

In more restrained terms the philosopher Nelson Goodman summarizes the dynamic function of a symbol. He writes:

We focus upon frontiers; the peak of interest in a symbol tends to occur at the time of revelation, somewhere midway in the passage from the obscure to the obvious. But there is endurance and renewal, too. Discoveries become knowledge only when preserved in accessible form; the trenchant and laden symbol does not become worthless when it becomes familiar, but is incorporated in the base for further exploration. And where there is density in the symbol system, familiarity is never complete and final; another look may always disclose significant new subtleties. Moreover what we read from and learn from a symbol varies with what we bring to it. Not only do we discover the world through our symbols but we understand and reappraise our symbols progressively in the light of our growing experience.[14]

But symbols are perhaps most dangerous when we are quite unaware of their existence. They tap unconscious mental energies and can thus be used for the highest educative and inspirational purposes—or they can be perverted for political and commercial

---

[12] *The Gutenberg Galaxy*, p. 31. '. . . we can transcend the limitations of our own assumptions by a critique of them. . . . The electro-magnetic discoveries have recreated the simultaneous "field" in all human affairs so that the human family now lives under conditions of a "global village". We live in a single constricted space resonant with tribal drums. So that concern with the "primitive" today is as banal as nineteenth-century concern with "progress", and as irrelevant to our problems.'

[13] Here, as elsewhere, I have tried to avoid discussion of 'myth'; not because it is unimportant, but because it is difficult. In my terms, however, a definition may be offered: a myth is the largely unconscious pattern in which symbols are articulated for a community.

[14] *The Languages of Art*, p. 259.

ends. A provisional criterion for testing the worth of particular symbols might be to ask a question about the balance between the imaginative and analytic modes of thought: are the symbols being used to quench rational thought or are they complementary to it? Theologically this might be regarded as an inadequate test. Nevertheless, as we turn to consider the difference between symbol and sacrament, it might be as well to consider the possibility that sacramental worship was only able to evolve from magic because there was a parallel and countervailing development of rational thought.

Sacrament. Against this hierarchy of signal and sign/symbol it may be possible to clarify the special meaning of the word 'sacrament'. I suggest a somewhat restricted definition which excludes theological words: a sacrament is *a special kind of symbol limited to collective acceptance and effect.* It transforms the community who accept it to a higher order of unity and action. Because it never has merely individual effects, a sacrament's meaning will elude individual description. If a Catholic were to explain, say the communion bread, to me, an individual Quaker, his words would explain a symbolic but not a sacramental meaning, though I might imagine myself as a Catholic and so get a theoretical glimpse of its higher meaning. The full meaning of a sacramental act can only be realized after personal experience, by the re-creation of the individual in his refreshed community—which for Christians is the Church.

This line of thought suggests an enlargement of the meaning of 'meaning' beyond that of relating an inner concept to a class of outer referents. When a sign is acting as a symbol, and even more if it is being effective as a sacrament, then its meaning refers *to possible events in the future and also to its power to act on people.* It changes those who utter it and those who hear. This is the main purpose of prayer, if seen at the level of psychology rather than of theology. In a strict sense the words of prayer are never used twice by the same person in quite the same way. They may be jangled repetitively, which is, I am afraid, what we mostly do. But if we use them with interest and meaning, then they will 'use' us. If the symbol leaves us, who use it, changed, it too will seem fresh next time. This pristine quality is also evident in poetry. Erwin Schrödinger expresses it thus:

> The real trouble is this: giving expression to thought by the observable medium of words is like the work of a silk-worm. In being made into silk the material achieves its value. But in the light of day it stiffens; it becomes something alien, no longer malleable. True we can then more easily and freely recall the same thought, but perhaps we can never experience it again in its original freshness. Hence it is always our latest and deepest insights that are the *voce meliora*.[15]

Seen in terms such as these language is never static. Concepts extend, and sometimes narrow, their boundaries. The meaning of words shift. Susanne Langer, developing the ideas of Cassirer and others, suggests that words first arose in the most primitive human communities alongside various rhythmical, ritual responses to such momentous events as a successful hunt or the return of spring. She then sees a subsequent tendency for words to become more precise and gradually to lose their symbolic quality. 'Speech', she suggests, 'becomes increasingly discursive, practical, prosaic, until human beings can actually believe that it was invented as a utility and was later embellished with metaphors for the sake of a cultural product called poetry.'[16] Both metaphor and poetry work in the contrary direction, for they can give words new and wider connotations and sometimes recharge them with the power characteristic of symbols.

It should not be assumed that Susanne Langer is suggesting that the element of communication was absent from primitive situations. People lagging in the chase might need to be informed that 'the hunt is over', but those most deeply involved would already know. What then, in general terms, do we conjecture was the main function of such hypothetical proto-language? Probably, as with children, it had a highly self-educative function: to prepare the appropriate attitudes and resilience in outlook which rapidly changing situations demanded from individuals, and to make the morale of the group strong. If this were so,

---

[15] *My View of the World*, p. 9.
[16] *Philosophy in a New Key*, p. 142.

language in its primitive stage served functions which combined those of sign, symbol, and sacrament.

I would suggest one further idea, that the feelings which charged many of these archaic words must have been ones which we associate much more with uncertainty than with certainty,[17] feelings of questioning, tension, and doubt as well as those of jubilation and satiety. Such feelings of uncertainty are entirely appropriate to 'frontier' situations as men and women occasionally experience them today, in self-imposed adventure, in artistic creation, in childbirth, in scientific discovery, or in the religious quest.[18]

Words, in origin, are action. A concept is like a very special skill and the sign that we make is its special artefact. Luria, the Russian psychologist, indicates this when he writes: 'The word . . . becomes a tremendous factor which forms mental activity, perfecting the reflection of reality and creating new forms of attention, of memory and imagination of thought and action'.[19]

[17] Malinowski, in *The Foundations of Faith and Morals*, p. 22, points out that the Trobriand Islanders only associate magic and myth with activities which are challenging, dangerous, or of doubtful outcome.

[18] J. Bronowski in *The Identity of Man*, Chs. II and III, shows how a scientist starts with a paradox and seeks to reduce its ambiguity; while a poet starts with a paradox and exploits its ambiguity.

[19] A. R. Luria and F. Yudovich, *Speech and the Development of Mental Processes in the Child*, p. 12.

6 Skills and potentialities

'Analyse your opponent's putting' is the golden rule. Ask him
what muscles he brings into play, and from what part of the body
'the sequence of muscular response' begins.
STEPHEN POTTER, *The Theory and Practice of Gamesmanship*

Anthropologists, psychologists, and archaeologists will no doubt
gradually discover a scientific equivalent of the Adam myth. In
this direction lie fascinating questions which the successors of
Lorenz and Leakey will eventually answer. Just how sudden was
the spurt of evolution which produced the human brain? Just
how much were speech, symbolization, and concept-forming the
results, or the causal concomitants, of this acceleration? How
much are we justified in postulating big genetic mutations in the
ascent of man? And was he primarily fighter or maker or
dreamer?

There is one kind of activity which runs right through this
evolutionary threshold, whose common elements still demand
much study and should be of continuing interest to teachers.
I refer to skills. They are found in the highest and, perhaps, in
the lowest of animals. In a crude sense they can be said to exist
in plants and even in some machines. Unconscious bodily processes have taken over the simpler, habitual skills; and now
machinery takes over others. But there have always been shifts
like this in the economy of skills. The effect of either biological
or industrial automation should be to enhance them and to
open up new ones.

It is difficult to classify or to isolate human skills. This may
be one reason why educationists sometimes treat them lightly as
though they were 'mere' technological accomplishments. 'We do
not call a person educated who has *simply* mastered a skill,'
writes R. S. Peters,[1] 'even though the skill may be a very worth-

[1] R. S. Peters, essay on 'The Philosophy of Education' in *The Study of
Education*, ed. Tibble, p. 73.

while one like that of moulding clay. For a man to be educated it is insufficient that he should possess *merely know-how* or *knack*. He must also know that certain things are the case.' I have italicized the words that appear to be putting skills in their place—in the craft room, along with the clay and the potter's wheel. But what of the skills of discernment, of testing and imagination which make men wonder if certain things really 'are the case', or to perceive them for the first time?

What is a skill? A good starting-point is in Michael Polanyi's *Personal Knowledge*.[2] Polanyi looks into the relationship between knowing and skilful doing. He starts from the fact that the highly organized activity which we call a skill is not normally understood in detail by the performer. He says:

I have come to the conclusion that the principle by which a cyclist keeps his balance while cycling [reasonably fast] is not generally known. The rule observed by the cyclist is this. When he starts falling to the right he turns his handlebars to the right, so that the course of the bicycle is deflected along a curve to the right. This results in a centrifugal force pushing the cyclist to the left and offsets the gravitational force dragging him down to the right. This manœuvre presently throws the cyclist out of balance to his left, which he counteracts by turning his handlebars to the left; and so he continues to keep himself in balance by winding along a series of appropriate curvatures. A simple analysis shows that for a given angle of unbalance the curvature of each winding is inversely proportional to the square of the speed ... But does this tell us exactly how to ride a bicycle? No. You obviously cannot adjust the curvature of your bicycle's path in proportion to the ratio of the unbalance over the square of the speed; and if you could you would fall off the machine, for there are a number of other factors ...

'Rules of art', says Polanyi, 'can be useful but they do not determine the art.' He takes many illuminating examples from connoisseurship, from medical diagnosis, from judicial procedure, and from music to show the wide truth of this maxim. He shows that a great deal of what we regard as our capacity to know, to learn, to act skilfully, depends on tacit knowledge—areas of

[2] Michael Polanyi, *Personal Knowledge*. Quotations are from Ch. IV.

competence below the level of unreflecting consciousness. Yet we learn to trust these, as we learn to trust ourselves. Polanyi accepts that 'destructive analysis', here as elsewhere, may yield useful information about skills and eliminate false explanations, but it cannot possibly provide the basis for effective learning. 'If a pianist shifts his attention from the piece he is playing to the observation of what he is doing with his fingers . . . he gets confused and may have to stop.' Later in the same chapter Polanyi makes some educational comments of considerable importance. 'To learn by example is to submit to authority. You follow your master because you trust his manner of doing things even when you cannot analyse and account in detail for its effectiveness. By watching the master and emulating his efforts in the presence of his example, the apprentice unconsciously picks up the rules of the art including those which are not explicitly known to the master himself. These hidden rules can be assimilated only by a person who surrenders to . . . the imitation of another. A society which wants to preserve a fund of personal knowledge must submit to tradition.'

So far therefore we have followed Polanyi in seeing skill as a complex of memories and actions focused by the attention of the performer. And there is now the further suggestion about their transmission, introduced by words like 'surrender' and 'submission to tradition'—words which will repel some readers. But what Polanyi means is that a learner must accept the continuing process of the craft as a whole. He must then learn it from within by sharing some of the high-level problems which face a skilled performer and by sharing the master's power to sketch out—to symbolize—their solution. Polanyi is not advocating submission to a crafts*man*, but to something much older—to a *craft*. This does not mean that in learning a complex skill one's critical or analytical powers should be suspended. These are useful both in the process of refining a skill after its main outlines have been absorbed and, to some extent, in its subsequent transmission. Where so many educational methods are at fault is that analysis and knowing 'what' are treated as primary when they should almost always follow extensive experience and knowing 'how'.

Polanyi develops some further ideas which started what was, to me, the helpful procedure of trying to envisage a skill with its time dimension strongly emphasized. He makes an important distinction between two kinds of awareness in regard to our own skilled actions: *subsidiary awareness*, which can remain un-conscious, and *focal awareness,* which is the fixing of attention on a series of objectives. 'When we use a hammer to drive in a nail, we attend to both nail and hammer, *but in a different way.* We *watch* the effect of our strokes on the nail and try to wield the hammer so as to hit the nail most effectively. When we bring down the hammer we do not feel that its handle has struck our palm but that its head has struck the nail. Yet in a sense we are certainly alert to the feelings in our palm though they are not watched in themselves; we watch something else while keeping intensely aware of them. I have a *subsidiary awareness* of the feeling in the palm of my hand which is merged into my *focal awareness* of my driving in the nail.'

If we now ask 'What is this focal awareness?' we will find that the answer must be stated in terms which involve guesses about the future. Doubtless the antecedents of every skilled act were in countless past movements, whose records are now sorted and stored in the brain. But now this experience is focused in anticipa-tion of the future. It is organized as a progressive whole, and if this whole is broken by my consciousness withdrawing in order to observe a part of it, then the skilled act is suspended. We noted earlier the similar break caused by the intrusion of a scientific observer on a performer who is at full stretch. But while it continues, focal awareness is unimpeded and we know, by subsequent reflection, that it attaches itself to an enormous number of points succeeding each other in time. A moment ago my eyes were fixed on the word 'an' in the previous sentence, but in my mind two images of rival words were alternating— 'infinite' and 'enormous'. Of course this focus of attention some-times sweeps much further ahead. Just now I was thinking of the links between chapters eight and nine, which I shall work on next week. Focal awareness is rather like the operation of a radar beam bouncing off near and far objects in a crowded harbour, which reduces the three-dimensional picture to a two-dimensional screen. But of course this probe of focal awareness reaches into a fourth dimension—the future—and relates what it finds to present information in the three-dimensional system of our brain.

Polanyi's subsidiary awareness, on the other hand, is discontinuous, and when we have such awareness, we have it here and now. The flow of information goes on throughout the brain and body, but we are only consciously aware of it when we break the skilled act and analyse it, looking for a fault perhaps or from curiosity.

We run into a difficulty at this point. It is reasonable to suppose that the past of a skill is recorded in the brain. But when I am actually thinking about the nail I am going to hit or the next chapter I am going to write, when my focal awareness is 'out there in the future'—where is it? To find an answer we must look from our two opposing viewpoints. If we could analyse the whole material of the brain which is relevant to nail-hitting or writing we would find the traces of many years of experience, but presumably we would also, in principle, be able to find certain patterns or tensions which we could point to and say: 'There it is—that complex swirl represents your anticipatory plans for the next second, or for the next week.' Of course we are very far from being able to do any such thing; nevertheless all our language and all our conceptual ways of thinking are geared to the assumption that our thoughts do penetrate the future. Though it may appear from a detached point of view that 'man's ability to articulate a future tense is a metaphysical scandal',[3] it is a scandal that we are quite happy to go on perpetrating most of the time. Similarly we continue to use skills and to impose a modest control on future events, acting as though skill gives us freedom. And this often works too.

It may help some, especially those who like to visualize, if we try to hold the past, present, and future of a skill together in the form of a diagram (Fig. 5). The large disc in the middle stands for all the cerebral and bodily circuitry and engineering which go to make up a skill at present. Let us assume that the skill in

[3] George Steiner, broadcast talk on 'Linguistic Origins'.

question is hammering. It has been shown on the disc as a branching system, though doubtless the lattice of connections in the brain is of a higher order than the tree-like structure here suggested.[4]

The past has also been suggested. Assume that Polanyi's joiner with the hammer is now thirty years old. Twenty years

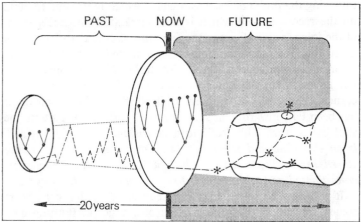

FIG. 5. Diagram suggesting the past, present, and future aspects of 'a skill'. The larger vertical disc represents the whole organism now. The fifteen dots on it stand for all the information items and for all cells and structures necessary for the working of a skill. The smaller disc represents these elements in the early stages of the skill's development, based on less co-ordinated information. The jagged line represents the billions of movements, acts, and explorations, occurring intermittently while the skill was being extended and improved. The stars suggest questions and guesses projected on to 'the future' by the more or less precise probing which Polanyi terms 'focal awareness' which accompanies a skill. The odd-shaped cone is the unique potential field with which a skill endows its possessor. One 'guess' is shown as an error, which, though near the limit of skill, goes beyond it. The cut-off at the right-hand edge is diagrammatic convention and not intended as the tragic nemesis from such an error. No scale relationship is intended between the disc, whose limits are those of a person's body, and the cone, whose limits are those of a person's activity.

[4] There is an interesting analogy here between the orderliness of a brain and the orderliness of a city. See Christopher Alexander, 'A City is not a Tree', *Architectural Forum*, April and May 1965, in which he contends that town planning has been handicapped by being based on tree patterns and not on the more complex semi-lattices which characterize medieval towns.

ago he was at his primary school and was receiving some formal instruction in how to use a hammer. Of course his experience was far less, having seen fewer examples of skilled action, made fewer mistakes, and achieved fewer successes. This situation is suggested by the simpler branching pattern on the left. The erratic line suggests the vast number of separate acts, always following the probe of focal awareness, which have gone to build up the record system which is now integrated into the pattern of the joiner's skill. For twenty years this skill pattern has grown from countless sources, from older craftsmen, from trial and error, and from success. Stroke by stroke this development has left its mark on the outer world too, in bent nails or perfect corners. Outwardly a temporal trail of slightly increased order has been left; inwardly, in some material and spatial pattern, the skill exists now. This leads to a provisional definition: *a skill is an elaborate and progressively refined pattern of experience stored in the brain, which when activated produces complex, co-ordinated acts whose aim is to effect changes in the future.*

It will now be seen that a skill, envisaged in this way, bears some similarities to our description of a concept. Both develop in a social and experiential setting, both must be represented by complex brain patterns, and both point to a field, edged with a penumbra of uncertainty, in the future. But there are important distinctions. Conceptual processes are almost entirely limited to human beings; skills are widespread throughout the animal kingdom.[5] Animal skills can apparently be both inherited and learned. They are refined at two levels: at the evolutionary level, which gives rise to instinctive skills, and at the level of learning, which, in the most complex skills, contributes a large proportion of the information required for precise estimates of distance, accurate timing, and foresight. It has been observed, for example, that newly fledged kingfishers in their first instinctive swoops for fish only score about one in twenty successes. Within a few weeks

[5] If we modify the definition by excluding any reference to the brain and allow for simpler forms of memory, we could include in it skills from the world of plants and machines. Cybernetic devices like guided missiles have simple skills built into them.

they polish their skill to match their parents' score of about one in three. But even here, the margin of error is considerable.

The reader may care to check some of these ideas against his own experience. In industrial society one of the commonest complex skills now being transmitted to adults is that of driving a car. Some degree of introspection, judiciously indulged in, can yield interesting illustrations. You may note the way in which focal awareness sweeps ahead down the road, gauging alternatives and margins, and you may discover that any self-praise, like Stephen Potter's muscular analysis, is liable to produce error. Somehow it breaks this future-directed flow of attention.

We will now consider the future-directed character of a skill in greater detail, its potentiality. This can lead to a deeper understanding of motivation. First, however, I propose to quote the testimony of a somewhat eccentric but brilliant rock-climber, the late J. M. Edwards, who made numerous difficult new ascents, many of them solitary ones, in the nineteen-thirties and forties. Rock climbing occupies an interesting intermediate position between a skill like driving and an artistic skill. In the former, one hopes that there will be no 'creativity'; in the climbing of new routes, however, there is a real element of originality though no artefact results. This is how Edwards describes such exploration:

The slope I took by stages. Three hundred yards, then a rest. . . . During each rest I gazed at the cliff, exploring from a distance how a route might go. Then when quite near the cliff I stopped again and looked up at it more slowly, heavy with fresh air, and it looked at me, and it slid about in the air as a cliff sometimes does, and was very difficult to focus. I shall go there and there, I thought, and then perhaps coming to the steeper portion, I shall go there, or perhaps it will be too hard for me to go there then I shall not go there but will go there instead by what appears to be so far as I can see from here to be a dirty bare sided finger crack, but which may not be so, or otherwise examining the rock closely when we are there, rubbing our nose against it, there may be some third or fourth way, not guessed at from a distance. But first, I thought, . . . I will rest here for a little time . . .[6]

[6] From *Samson, the Life and Writings of Menlove Edwards*, ed. Sutton and Noyce.

Here Edwards is describing an important aspect of rock-climbing skill. It corresponds, at a lower level, to the scientist's imaginative power to create hypotheses. The climber sketches out a flexible, mental structure of branching alternatives which become his programme of action. Later in his essay Edwards describes how he did not get up and it was characteristic of him that he could analyse failure but not success. 'I am fifteen feet from the ground on easy rocks but in my bones there is no more energy than there ever was and my whole soul is as flat as a carpet, what am I to do? Perhaps if I were to recall former victories or to picture glory, but how can you do that when you are alone? Now if there were an onlooker that would make the effort worth while . . .'

There is no doubt that what Edwards calls 'glory', meaning general social approval, is a factor which helps to provide the motive for difficult actions. But I suspect that it becomes less and less important as mastery of skills increases. Many educational devices make use of this—mark lists, prize giving, etc., but Edwards's own life suggests that, for him, this 'glory' was relatively unimportant. He was ruggedly independent, often climbed alone, refused military service during the war. His remarks about recalling former victories and his soul being flat point, albeit somewhat vaguely, to the two main internal sources from which high-level skills draw their motivation. One is retrospective and the other is prospective. By introducing the term 'high-level skills' I am suggesting that we must search beyond the satisfactions of hunger and sex and look at more specifically human attributes as we seek to understand why people enjoy exercising their most developed skills at frontier limits which are often arduous and apparently unrewarding.

The first internal source of motive is what Edwards referred to as 'past victories'. Much animal and human learning can be strengthened by the use of 'reinforcements'. This means rewards and satisfactions which are given, or found, on the successful completion of a task. As a person matures and becomes more and more a master of his particular skill, external reinforcements appear to become less important and the recollection of past efforts and successes become more so. When I was twelve I positively disliked the sensation of sweat trickling down into my eyes as I made my way up a warm Alpine path; today I would enjoy it. 'Masochism' murmers my Freudian friend, and I only half believe it, for scores of such journeys now blend in my memory (the path to Pillar, the gentians by the path to the Glockner . . .) and the sweat cannot be separated from many friendships, the peace, and the thin air of success.

In Edwards's account the working of another motive, subtler than material rewards, can be discerned. It is more to do with the unknown than the known, more with the future than the past. Edwards describes its operation as he formulates numerous possibilities of prospective action. It is the state of *potentiality* with which a skill endows us. The immediate feeling which it gives is a balanced sense of competence and of curiosity. The more generalized power is that of having in the imagination possible solutions and hypotheses which carry with them the wish to test them. This is I think analogous to the very simplest cybernetic 'skills', like a guided missile with 'don't go off till . . .' instructions programmed in it. When its radar or other sensory system reports that there is a massive object within range, it will explode or change course according to the instructions which it carries. Norbert Wiener makes illuminating comment on such mechanical devices: 'Not only', he writes, 'can we build purpose into machines, but in an overwhelming majority of cases a machine designed to avoid certain pitfalls . . . *will look for purposes which it can fulfil.*'[7] At a vastly higher level a human skill charges its possessor with a special tension, a readiness and desire to try it out again.

Success in rock climbing or in many other complex and exacting skills requires a subtle combination of these two elements:

[7] Wiener, *The Human Use of Human Beings*, p. 36 (my italics). This book is a popular version of his *Cybernetics.* One can note other interesting parallels between the learning of machines and of animals and men. As learning gets more complex it becomes hierarchical. Gombrich in his *Art and Illusion* (p. 88) draws attention to this and quotes a striking description of learning as 'an arboriform stratification of guesses about the future'. Tree patterns certainly are suggestive, but see note on p. 55.

past victories play their part in establishing the confidence that 'there is a way . . .', while imagination tempers this with the conditional or subjunctive mood to complete the sentence— '. . . if only I can find it'. That these are separate aspects of motivation may be illustrated by what happens when they are not in balance. In mountaineering, excess of the thrusting element soon leads the climber into predicaments beyond the safe limits of his skill, while excess of imagination leaves him with many possible lines but with no 'will' to achieve them.

I shall now propose a mental extension to my earlier diagram which may help us to envisage the future-directed or potential aspect of skills. When trying to conceptualize Polanyi's notion of focal awareness we were forced to introduce a time element into our picture. When we apply this to a particular skill like climbing it becomes evident that the future of the skill has a 'shape'. I use this spatial word metaphorically, though we might use other phrases like 'unique character'. The spatial metaphor has value in emphasizing the several dimensions of a skill. One man's skill has a particular, unique history, though it may grow within a larger field of tradition. In the present it must have a coded, material substrate in the brain tissues—presumably a unique pattern. In the future this can be conceptually extrapolated as a field of potential action and this too is, or will be, unique. When Edwards mentally sketched out a range of alternative routes on the cliff, he was doing so mainly within the limits of his own field, though of course some of his 'possibilities' might, when tested, have proved just beyond this limit. As he developed his skill, year after year, the field of his potential also grew larger and his capacity for guessing its limits accurately would also become more precise. Here again we see the interaction of the thrusting and imagining components. This 'shape' gradually becomes more characteristic of the skilled man himself, of his style. Even today when I walk up by the Devil's Kitchen above Lake Ogwen, I look up at the steep grey wall on the right, with its thin grass ledges, and say: 'Yes, typical Edwards country, but not my kind of climbing.' This unique personal stamp on work is even more evident in the achievement of creative artists than with explorers or athletes. An artist will possess large resources of skill which he shares in common with others, but round the edges of his field, where he is operating near his limit, he will be actively stretching and shaping his own individual perimeter.

In developing these ideas on a diagrammatic basis (p. 55) my aim has been to hold together the 'was' and the 'is' and the 'might be' of skills. As we have seen, it is not only skills that can be better understood if the dimension of time is strongly emphasized. This is true of words, works of art, and of the people who 'utter' them. Of course a diagram like this is a caricature. It emphasizes relationship by vastly distorting scale. But it should be able to stand up to this test: *that each bit refers to the relationship of things to patterns at some time.* For instance, whatever changes occur in my brain as I cross this 't' would be represented by shifts in the 15 dots of the tree pattern as these stand for all the billions of particles in my brain and sensory and motor systems relevant to the skill under discussion.

We have come to see that a skill is one of those special 'things', like living organisms and words and works of art, which change themselves, which change their environment, their observers, and their users, as they pass through time. They operate in opposition to chaos, to what is unpredictable, pushing it back a little and thereby encompassing small enclaves of what we call freedom.[8]

The next chapter will touch on some of the difficulties which speculation about freedom and causation must raise. Does a skill increase our freedom? An old paradox begins to emerge, one from which a greater knowledge of skills and motivation may not free us, though it may loosen its grip. A skill, whether human or animal or even mechanical, always relates present action to guesses about the future. This means that future uncertainties (probabilities) are programmed as present causes.

This is true of the most precise skills. The focal awareness of an architect, for instance, plays over his envisaged plans for a building to be completed in three years' time. He is using his

---

[8] I first developed this concept of skills having a past, present, and future component in 'Skills and Safety', *The Climbers Club Journal*, 1962.

skilled intelligence, operating on as wide a basis of generality as possible, so that future hypothetical possibilities can guide his pencil and inform his arithmetic. It is of course a characteristic power of humans that the point of focal awareness can be pushed out much further than with animals.[9] Our language, our science, and many of our most complex technical skills combine, sometimes with success, but often not, to extend this realistic grip on future 'events'. Hubris is to think this can be done without sufficient built-in doubt. 'We are saved', writes George Eliot, 'by making the future present to ourselves.'[10]

[9] There are interesting paths to be explored in the territory where Polanyi's ideas interlock with McLuhan's, and these might have important educational applications. Briefly: when a person is exercising a skill his focal awareness (future directed) unites all relevant brain and body material in a confluent, branching system. But when he stops to think or talk about the skill, subsidiary awareness of its component parts is attained by retrospection and analysis. Moreover, such awareness will usually be expressed and communicated in linear form. Put cryptically: what a teacher hopes to transmit is a tree of knowledge; what he generally succeeds in transmitting is a chain.

[10] George Eliot, *Felix Holt,* p. 244.

7 Time and personality

There are three times, a present of things past, a present of things present, a present of things future. For these three exist in the mind and I find them nowhere else.

ST. AUGUSTINE, *Confessions*, Bk. 11, § xx

In the first three chapters I have tried to sketch an epistemology which sought the meaning of 'knowing' mainly in the process of getting to know. This process of enlargement is at the heart of all creative work and of all effective education. But this book is a pedestrian's reconnaissance, not an attempt at high-level philosophical charting. So, with this licence, if it is a licence, we plunged into three areas where other more specialist explorers have been at work, and we looked at their ideas on dreams, concepts, and skills. We tried to understand some of the different ways in which a person comes to perceive patterns of order in the face of seeming disorder, doubt and danger. In the chapters which follow we shall consider certain puzzling, yet commonplace matters which may appear clearer when seen as process rather than as state or thing. These are: the growing person of a child—his freedom, motivation, and vocation—and the encounter between young and old. What then is this boy who sits a little aloof from the others, non-communicative, with a wise but timid look? What is he; who is he?[1] One moment he is an 'it'—our problem; the next he seems like the embodiment of an ancient past, carrier of life and spirit to an unlimited future. The traditional concept of a human soul was capable of holding this 'it' and this 'thou' in fruitful tension. Even today, if we can ignore the overtones of the word 'soul', its suggestions of ego-survival, of ghosts and houris, and hold on to its central meaning, we may

---

[1] St. Augustine in *The Confessions* (Bk. 10) asks similar questions, *'Who* am and *what* am I?'

still find that it can help us to face one another with more charity and patience than is common.

This central area of meaning points to both the past and future of a person in a manner which other words like 'self' fail to do. Yet if one were to mention a child's soul, casually, in a school staff-room it would almost certainly cause embarrassment, unless one could turn it off as a joke. This is an interesting state of affairs, because almost every really effective teacher, whether humanist, catholic, or communist in outlook, treats children as if they were spiritual entities, as if they were able to use freedom, and as if they were capable of expressing and disseminating truth, love, and beauty for future generations. In discussion we resemble inverted Victorians and keep our religious words rather than our sex words under a taboo. Nevertheless, it is doubtful if an adequate concept of education can be gained unless we try to view the whole process *sub specie aeternitatis,* or at least in the perspective of very long epochs. To see a person in depth is to see him now in terms of his past and to see him now in terms of his future and of the race's future. This concept of time was first articulated by St. Augustine and, though today it is unfashionable, it is highly relevant to our line of thought. As Marjorie Grene points out in *The Knower and the Known*: 'If knowing is one of the kinds of activity perfected by living persons, then we need . . . an adequate conception of activity . . . a tenable theory of action as responsible and free'; but she also warns us that, though the metaphysics of time is perilous, 'yet it can give us tools for solving philosophical riddles which all the efforts of rationalism are unable to disentangle'.[2]

When we look at our friend as a Thou, we find that our imagination and feelings travel beyond the interesting armour of skin and hair. These surfaces, soft like a peach perhaps, or lizard-wrinkled, are not the centres of our love. Essentially we care for those patterns of a person's being which show in speech, expression, and gesture, whose activity we recognize as mind, and whose meaning reaches out into the future. If we have confidence in a person it is because we believe that there is some correspondence

[2] Marjorie Grene, op. cit., p. 252.

between what is and what might be, between promise and performance. And this implies the possibility of failure and also the belief, perhaps irrational, that each individual moves in a field of choice. *Seen thus a person is his potentialities; he is the unique shape of his freedom.*

Even the simplest animal skills contain an element of anticipation, of choice, a waiting till the right moment. When we turn to consider a human being in terms of past, present, and future, we see him as a vast bundle of 'skills', all of which are grounded and summarized in the brain, but all of which create complex fields of potentiality which seem to fan out into the future like the beam of an electric torch or the cone of our own vision. All the conceptual apparatus of language and art share this four-dimensional, time-penetrating, open-ended, anticipatory character. It will be clear that, in trying to avoid using the big word 'soul' which does have as its centre a four-dimensional time-embracing connotation, I am falling back on a three-dimensional model which can be reduced even further to my two-dimensional skill diagram. But whether we use the religious word, the visual image of the electric torch or the diagram of the cone or all three, the intention is the same: to reinstate a sense of time at the centre of our concept of a person, and with it a sense of individual freedom. We shall turn to this in greater detail in the next chapter, not with any notion of answering an ancient riddle, but to show that our scientific understanding of people in general need not be determinist and does not run counter to our intuition that, when we care for an individual, we are caring for his freedom.

We all find ourselves in this paradoxical situation, that we know—through experience as well as precept—that we must try to treat people as though a path of freedom stretched before each one; yet we also know, as we look back on our own and mankind's history, that we can uncover an unlimited network of causes and causes behind causes. Each process seems part of a bigger one. I do not doubt that the main development of living organisms is evolutionary and that either as individuals or as large groups we are involved in it. But evolution is not a simple machine-like process. Many problems about its mode of operation still remain unsolved. As the search continues for an adequate theory of human activity and motivation, three points should be borne in mind: First, we should not be searching for a complete break in the thread of evolution, though the possibility of unusually rapid change should not be excluded. Second, though there may not be a difference in kind between a machine and a man (the basic stuff can be the same in both) nevertheless the difference in complexity is so enormous as to lead us to expect the behaviour of this stuff to be different. Thirdly, it appears that the more complex the organism the more important becomes the transmission and interpretation of information. (Readers who have kept abreast of developments in biochemistry during the past fifteen years may care to skip the next paragraph.)

Statistics may bemuse, but they also set a scale. There are about 1,000 million nerve cells in a man's brain. The largest computer yet built has one ten-thousandth of this number of units and each of these is far cruder than a neurone. The general growth of the human brain, the most complex thing in the world, follows the lines specified in the nucleus of the cell created at the embryo's conception. Just how this development is guided and just how specific the information is, still remain mysteries. Again, almost every cell nucleus in the whole body (some, like red-blood cells, must be excluded) contains the same library of information in long twists of code-carrying DNA. It is said that if you untwisted all the DNA in the ten thousand million cells of one man's body, the strands would stretch across the solar system! This sounds a somewhat laborious undertaking, though it might provide a suitable penance for anyone who says 'nothing but' about molecules. Nevertheless, this DNA does apparently, in a marvellous manner, embrace the evolution of our planet. It is a condensed record of the evolution of life during thousands of millions of years of continuity. There can have been few major happenings in the solar system which have not made their mark in this vast library of the chromosomes. Nor is this record only in the summary, linear language of the DNA. It can be perceived in more diffuse form in all our tissues and in the rhythmical patterns through which they act. D'Arcy Thompson, writing long before the discovery of DNA, puts it thus: 'In the marble columns and architraves of a Greek temple we still trace the timbers of its wooden prototype, and see beyond these the tree trunks of a sacred grove; roof eaves of a pagoda recall the sagging mats which roofed an earlier edifice . . . So we see enduring traces of the past in living organisms—landmarks which have lasted on through altered functions and altered needs; and yet at every stage new needs are met and new functions effectively performed.'[3]

If now, for a moment, we can hold in mind the picture of a single human cell, just fertilized, about to undergo its first mitosis, we have the limiting case of a human existence. It illuminates clearly the three 'times' which St. Augustine refers to in his introspection quoted at the beginning of the chapter. The vast, causal network of time past is concentrated in the information of the chromosomes. But the meaning of this unique message, 'written' in the chromosome, is in the future. It is the life and influence of a human soul. Here again we are trying to view a material pattern with binocular vision, with an analytical probe towards the past and with an imaginative beam towards the future. Whether these patterns are coded at this instant in the summary, linear statements of DNA, or whether they branch and burgeon in the active, rhythmical efflorescence of the phenotype, they are humanity and they are, in summary form, earth's ancient wisdom, harmony, discord, and incompleteness. They are, in St. Augustine's sense, the future too.

A THEOLOGICAL ASIDE

One of the gifts which science offers is a sense of our dependence, not only on each other but on the acts of men, animals and metazoa, long ago.[4] To know that we human beings culminate

[3] D'Arcy Thompson, *On Growth and Form*, Vol. 2 of complete edition, pp. 1020–1.

[4] I use the word 'act' here in the sense suggested by Susanne Langer in *Mind, an Essay on Human Feeling*. It would be foolish to suppose that animals have much freedom in their acts, but Susanne Langer here suggests an enlargement of the normal connotation of 'act' to cover all the 'process-things' in nature and especially those complex units which constitute

thousands of millions of years of evolution, and now also guide this process, gives rise to feelings of awe and responsibility. Here science and religion join.

At that phrase, 'also guide this process', we swing up to the creative frontier of the present, from what is in principle capable of analysis to what is of the future and can only be guessed and symbolized. To attain the sense of reverence, unity, and rooted-ness is certainly a big part of spiritual wisdom, and yet this is where the strictly scientific humanist must stop. In practice of course many humanists do venture over to the 'religious' side and are prepared to reflect in a quasi-religious way on natural symbols and on human potentiality, though they would reject the use of religious words like 'soul'. Occasionally, however, they betray the need for words of even higher generality as when C. H. Waddington writes: 'What we should be aiming at is that ethical principles should be subject to . . . some . . . supra ethical cri-terion.'[5] Should such a vast 'criterion' ever take on any conceptual shape in Waddington's or in any other humanist's mind, it is difficult to see how he would react to it in any way but what a theist would call 'worship'.

If Christians and others of religious mind are to develop an attitude and a conceptual framework which does not repel such friendly incursions from scientific humanists, our religious words must be sparing and should not appear to deny truth in any other field. We may be right to use the word God less than our forbears, and such reticence about the word can be a condition for redis-covering its meaning. Its area of reference is the total pattern and potential of the universe, not seen, never comprehended by its parts. For some people this whole is given a focus, meaning, and direction in Christ.[6] I cannot write anything that is likely to enlarge the connotation of words like God or Christ for anyone.

life's activity. She sees *feeling* as the animal's awareness of action and conscious thought as a narrow, specifically human segment in the spectrum of feeling.

[5] 'The Human Animal', an essay in *The Humanist Frame,* ed. Julian Huxley, p. 78.

[6] Teilhard de Chardin's *Phenomenon of Man* is now the classic exposi-tion of this view.

But lines of thought like those which have been drawn together in this book point below superficial misunderstandings to areas of shareable doubt. We cannot explain or prove this sense that there is spirit and freedom in the universe. Nor can we prove that this solitary child beams freedom and potentiality towards the future. We can act on these assumptions.[7]

[7] This image of a beam of freedom or the corresponding model of a skill which projects a cone of enhanced activity running forward through time is not as fanciful as it might appear. Similar imagery is being used by biologists in their attempts to understand the fields which shape and give direction to cell development and evolution. C. H. Waddington uses the term 'chreod' to denote such a morphogenetic field. *Towards a Theoretical Biology*, ed. Waddington, vol. 1, pp. 1–32, and especially the comments on this by René Thom, p. 40.

8 A kind of freedom

The little girl who said, 'it ain't my fault it's my glands' ' illustrates the fallacy which arises from confusing the dual aspects of a unity with cause and effect.

D. M. MACKAY, *Man as Mechanism*[1]

During the last thirty years many teachers must have rejected either through obstinacy or insight, the idea that children's abilities can be predicted with accuracy. Even at the height of the fashion for intelligence-testing we were inclined to work on the assumption that the tests were partial and inefficient and, though we might make use of them, we would rejoice when a child flouted their predictions. But educational interest in this field has shifted and deepened.

It is now generally recognized that though a child's I.Q. is one interesting, measurable dimension of its personality there are many others which affect intellectual performance. The work of Liam Hudson has taught us to distinguish between 'convergers'— those who do well in the single-answer type of test and 'divergers' —those who excell in open-ended problems requiring a rich imaginative response rather than logic and speed. The divergers gravitate towards the arts, the convergers towards science. But the divergers do not appear as clear-cut creative heroes in Hudson's drama. In discussing creativity he is rightly cautious, remarking that 'like many other virtues it is as difficult to disapprove of as to say what it means'.[2] Nevertheless he makes it clear that in the vicinity of this word lie many of the problems which are of greatest concern to educational theory. Yet they easily get misted in cliché.

The platitudes which ache to be released from this complex literature are the ones about the original scientist being the scientist who

[1] From *Christianity in a Mechanistic Universe*, edited by D. M. MacKay, p. 61.

[2] Liam Hudson, *Contrary Imaginations*.

possesses some of the divergent qualities of the artist; and the successful artist being the one who enjoys some of the rigour and dedicated single-mindedness of the scientist. This notion accords well with Kuhn's analysis of scientific invention—that it depends upon a tension between the forces of tradition and revolution. I am convinced [this] is applicable to the arts as well.[3]

This distinction parallels, in social-historical terms, the one that we have been using in this book, tradition turning to what is known, past, and analysable, revolution turning to what is unprecedented yet may be imagined and symbolized.

Perhaps new concepts of tradition and of transforming freedom need to be assimilated into our educational thinking. If this is so then some important philosophical/scientific problems must be acknowledged, even if they cannot be solved. It is here that the work of D. M. MacKay seems to offer an important cluster of ideas. He is a physicist and communications theorist who has turned his attention to some of the logical problems arising from the assumption of a mind/body unity.

MacKay starts with his feet firmly planted on the ground of the physical sciences and of Christianity and he explores man's mental/bodily unity from two sides. His ideas have a profound importance, not only for psychology and theology, but also for jurisprudence and education. His crucial argument is developed from the time-honoured problem that if a group of scientific onlookers knew the position and state of every particle in your brain they should, in theory, be able to predict your future actions. They could, for example, forecast whether your answer would be 'yes' or 'no' when, at seven o'clock this evening, you are to be offered a lift to the station. But, says MacKay, there is an important built-in complication to all such situations. The onlookers must decide whether to include in your brain knowledge about the experiment that is going on. If they deprive you of this information (and to do so would make their experiment scientifically more objective) they are reducing your status by reducing the scope of your information. If, on the other hand, they intend to tell you about the experiment and of the

[3] Liam Hudson, op. cit., p. 119.

prediction they arrive at, then the state of affairs which they are forecasting may itself be changed.[4] We are tied, according to MacKay in an intriguing logical knot and he asks:

What if the prediction that the scientific onlooker writes on the paper refers to the part of your brain which at the moment is, so to speak, lying blank waiting to receive the prediction? If he wants to write something you would be correct to believe, he is then in a very tough logical dilemma. For whatever he writes on the paper, your believing it would change your brain in such a way that it no longer corresponded to the description.[5]

And elsewhere MacKay sums up his argument with the words: 'To us, our choice is logically indeterminate, until we make it. For us choosing is not something to be observed or predicted but to be done;' or, 'It is people, not propositions, who are certain.'[6]

In reflecting on the paragraph quoted above, I am intrigued by that 'blank space' which MacKay metaphorically postulates. If you are going to try to keep an open mind about whether to go or wait at seven o'clock this evening, there must be some mechanism at work in your brain which is capable of sustaining this indeterminacy for a time. Seen from the side of introspection and mind this 'mechanism' appears as awareness of present doubt and impending decision. But looking at the same idea objectively, one can imagine a future brain scientist isolating some unusually complex circuit which would hold, like a coiled spring, a tension of doubt. Perhaps he might have to explain that its very removal from its context would destroy its essential quality. These last speculative sentences are not meant as science fiction

---

[4] In a comment on the preceding sentences Professor MacKay suggests that I have not stressed the central logic of his argument sufficiently. He writes: 'Whether or not they deprive you of this information, the key question is whether you would be *correct* to accept it as inevitable if you did know it. If not, then for you it does not count as true information (since you would be mistaken to believe it), and it offers no determinate alternative to your belief that your choice is still indeterminate.'

[5] MacKay, op. cit., p. 63.

[6] 'On the logical indeterminacy of a free choice', *Mind*, vol. lxix, no. 273, Jan. 1960, pp. 33 and 35.

but to emphasize that no supernatural entity is being assumed in this account of the roots of mental freedom.

Much of our language has evolved round man's special capacity for holding the options open. When you say 'I might go at seven o'clock' some mechanism in your brain maintains a 'space' of relative indeterminacy for a time. Experience has probably taught you that new information, different causal chains, can be brought into the decision if you wait. The choice you make is between the quality of causes you allow to operate. MacKay stresses that 'it is a question of freedom to change rather than freedom to choose; *of freedom to become different from what you are . . .*'[7] You either decide early on the basis of fewer bits of information or later on the basis of more. You assume, not necessarily correctly, that 'later' is likely to mean 'better'.

The whole apparatus of subjective grammar seems designed to allow this enrichment of our response by delay. Here it seems we have a parallel with symbolism. A symbol allows two or more conceptual areas to overlap for a period, until such time as the mind is capable of grasping an extended, unifying concept.[8] With ideas of a very comprehensive nature this time may never come. Our doubting, questioning mood, and the grammar that goes with it, allow alternative lines of possible action to coexist until the optimum, or necessary, time for decision comes. Both are devices for maintaining limited vistas of freedom in the pressing crowd of causes.

MacKay sees his conclusions as opening the way for a more unitary Christian faith. He sums up his Eddington Lecture as follows:

I am suggesting that fears of mechanistic explanations of brain function are groundless, not because we can be sure that the brain is not a machine, but even if it were, the whole constellation of claims

[7] *Freedom of Action in a Mechanistic Universe,* p. 35 (my italics).

[8] Since writing this I have read Marjorie Grene's *The Knower and the Known.* She quotes, p. 173, F. J. J. Buytendijk, *Mensch und Tier,* where he describes the attitude of a chimpanzee to tools: 'If the branch is used by a chimpanzee as a pole, it is no longer a branch, and therefore the pole is not, for him, a true tool. *Only for man are things equivocal*' (my italics).

regarding our inner nature and significance and destiny expressed in our moral tradition and in the Christian religion would remain unaffected. It is not people, but brains, that may or may not be machines. It is not brains, but people, that choose freely or otherwise, and in so doing determine their eternal destiny.[9]

I suspect that important implications for MacKay's ideas can be found in less exalted disciplines than theology. There may be fallacies still hidden in MacKay's exposition of this problem, but he seems to have indicated just the kind of logical process which would underlie the birth and growth of concepts, and even skills, as, following Cassirer and Langer, I have sketched in this book. The pattern produced is generally asymmetrical in time, being causal in retrospect and free in prospect. In origin such patterns are more to do with controlled doubts than with clear certainties. Taken all together they endow each person with a field of freedom and responsibility which is as uniquely his as his genes.

The concept of person as a complex bundle of all his past acts and present 'skills'[10] is central to this way of thinking. It is a very old concept but it needs to be rediscovered and reinterpreted.[11] One of its consequences is that it forces us to look in alternate directions while holding on to the unique concept of each person whom we know. We can be genuinely interested in all the details of his past traumas (or triumphs) and see them reflected in present problems; but if we also have a strong conviction that this person's essence is directed to the future and only fully attains meaning there, we will be less likely to speak and act as though what is is all.

While this way of looking at things may make it easier for us to be aware of our scientific-analytic role as well as of our complementary imaginative role in dealing with human beings and human situations, it does not in any way diminish the scope of science. Consider again the skill diagram (p. 55). Those fifteen

[9] MacKay, *Freedom of Action in a Mechanistic Universe*, p. 38.

[10] Here I am using skills in the large sense which I have suggested above. In this 'stretched' sense, language is man's super skill with words its tools.

[11] Marjorie Grene's *A Portrait of Aristotle* discusses the contemporary relevance in biology and human sciences of his ideas about actuality and potentiality. See also works by F. C. Copleston and others on Aquinas.

dots on the central disc of the present stand for the incredibly complex microcosm which is the objective fact of a person now. This, strictly speaking, is all that physiologists or purely scientific psychologists should be dealing with. In their research they are looking for, and will doubtless discover, patterns in this material which correspond to much of the present and past activity of the body. There is no reason why they should not eventually come to recognize qualitative variations. We already assume that in this material microcosm there will be perceptible discords and qualitative failings. The work of psychotherapists and priests is aimed, somehow, at healing these, though in any strict scientific sense we do not yet know what they are. Presumably the patterns of a saint or a genius would show harmonies which would be absent in other men. The difficulty might then arise that 'ordinary' observers would fail to read the patterns.

9 Motivation and the sense of purpose

> Strange, that some of us, with quick alternate vision, see beyond our infatuations, and even while we rave on the heights, behold the wide plains where our own persistent self awaits us.
>
> GEORGE ELIOT, *Middlemarch*[1]

Professor Waismann concludes a paper called 'Language Strata'[2] with the following:

An action may be viewed as a series of movements caused by some physiological stimuli in the 'only rats, no men' sense; or as something that has a purpose and meaning irrespective of the way its single links are produced. An action in the first sense is determined by causes, an action in the second sense by motives or reasons. . . . What we must understand is that the word 'action' has a systematic ambiguity. And yet we are continually invited to regard motives as a special sort of causes [*sic*]; perhaps because we have only one word 'why?' to ask for cause and motive.

This sums up the 'two-views-of-one-process' theme whose educational implications we have been exploring. It also draws attention to the ambiguity of the term 'an action'. Because an action is a process with duration it can be understood both by asking questions appropriate to its appearance before and after—before and

---

[1] The whole passage in *Middlemarch*, where Lydgate recalls the moment when he first knew that he would be a doctor, is worth studying (pp. 138–48). See also George Eliot's own intuitive perception of her first novel: 'one morning as I was lying in bed . . . my thoughts merged themselves into a dreamy doze, and I imagined myself writing a story of which the title was—"the Sad Fortunes of the Reverend Amos Barton"' (G. S. Haight, *George Eliot*, p. 206). Another remarkable example was the sense of vocation acquired by the great naturalist, Sir Joseph Banks, wandering along the river bank near Eton. He got his first science lesson from the gipsies (H. C. Cameron, *Sir Joseph Banks*, Ch. I).

[2] A paper originally delivered to the Jowett Society, Oxford, reprinted in *Logic and Language*, 2nd series, ed. A. G. N. Flew, pp. 30–1.

after we have done the action or been affected by it. The psychologists who study animal behaviour use experimental techniques which more or less eliminate this subjective but interesting ambiguity.[3] This does not mean that the work of behaviourists has no light to throw on human problems, but rather that it attains its value only when used to complement the insights gained by the doer who anticipates and experiences action. Indeed this other, 'upper'[4] side should be given priority. If it is correct that the gap between men and animals can best be understood in terms of man's achievements in the field of tool, concept, and symbol, then it is this field, rather than that of animal behaviour, that is likely to yield the most fertile ideas about the springs of human action.

We need to be wary of the noun 'motive', as it too easily implies that our interest is in a thing, like a stick or a carrot. In his book *The Concept of Motivation*,[5] R. S. Peters steps into this trap. 'The concept of "motivation" ', he suggests, 'has developed from that of motive.' Most of his examples are trivial, like crossing the road to buy tobacco, or they are rule-bound, like signing a contract or going through the ceremony of marriage. Professor Peters does not consider larger and less restricted acts like crossing an ice cap, building up a business, or falling in love. A schoolmaster soon learns that, though it is often a good idea to say 'what is your motive?' or 'let us clarify our aim', these goals have a curiously ephemeral quality. Part of the art of teaching is undoubtedly to share with the young in the creation and pursuit of interesting objectives; but many of the goals which generate

[3] *Motivation*, an anthology by Bindra and Stewart, provides a concise survey of the development of behaviourist experiment and theory.

[4] I use this evaluative term partly because Waismann suggests such a stratification but also because it seems capable of justification. See Polanyi's *Tacit Dimension*, p. 33, where he makes the case for treating a thing as more real, not because it is solid, but because it is highly organized and open to more possibilities of development. Thus a mind is more real than a stone.

[5] p. 28. Though most of Peters's examples are trivial and his conclusions are correspondingly restricted, he does stress at the end of the book that explanations in purely scientific—'Galilean'—terms are likely to be inadequate.

most thought and energy change, enlarge, and recede—like mirages. For this reason the process of motivation may be more readily understood than the abstraction.

In Chapter 5 we have suggested the close relationship between skills, uncertainty, and goals. In Chapter 8 we examined Mac-Kay's concept of the logical indeterminacy of responsible choice. We found here, as elsewhere, that some forms of human action take on contrasting appearances when viewed before or after. This 'asymmetry' in time is always marked when actions are of a transforming kind. Symbols, operating to enlarge a concept, showed this characteristic. Before the symbolic insight dawned there was contradiction; afterwards there was a unifying pattern. The 'subjunctive tension' which keeps the options open before a free decision is taken, displayed it. Before the decision there was a sense of freedom; after it, the causal pattern was evident. We should not be surprised to find a similar asymmetry in the process of human motivation.

THE THRESHOLD OF MANHOOD

The ideas that I shall put forward grew partly from the experience of educating adolescent boys at Abbotsholme. While not undervaluing formal methods of academic study we believed in the importance of aesthetic education, of drama, of adventurous outdoor pursuits, and in a variety of personal research and service projects. These convictions, which most staff and parents shared, were partly the result of a liberal tradition in the school. But they were also under constant critical review by articulate staff and parents and by frequently outspoken boys. Thus a steady process of experimental change was generated—not scientific experiment with the knowing ones outside, but the joint doubting and searching which characterizes an open society. Against this background, during twelve years at Abbotsholme, my colleagues and I developed certain general theories about what we were trying to do. Some were obvious. That, for example, the greatest gain from all the demanding but informal activities was that they brought teachers and learners together in situations where joint enterprise and mutual understanding could happen far more readily than in the classroom. I shall have more to say about this in the next chapter.

The age of boys at Abbotsholme ranged from 11 to 18. We recognized that most of the problems affecting pre-adolescent boys were concerned with feelings of security and that these pointed back to childhood. When an eleven-year-old feels that the large 'lap' of a school community is one that he can cope with as well as his mother's lap and home, he is ready to move ahead and is only one stage away from coping with the wider adult community. Most children found their feet quickly, though a few floundered and needed special help. When boarding schools fail in this respect they are, in my opinion, seriously at fault and may do more harm than incompetent day schools. But when a boarding school is reasonably competent and sympathetic in its dealings with children it can be extremely helpful in giving them confidence for the changes of adolescence. This is not the place to discuss the parallel problems and relative merits of single-sex and coeducational schools. It so happened that I found myself in a liberal and unusually lively boys' school where teachers and parents were all involved in learning. Here we had to think, and often act, about motivation problems.

The hopes and fears of normal adolescents tend to cluster round one central, unconscious question: What am I becoming? This is, I believe, a more acute question for boys than for girls. The main reason for this is that the image of the mother as a creative person, though blurred by pictures of cheesecake, career girls, and the standardized values of glossy magazines, does remain fairly strong in popular thinking. The image of what a man should be is a good deal less clear and less influential in present-day western society.

Most of the usual sexual anxieties of adolescents fit into the framework of this central question. Formerly they were sometimes twisted to produce a damaging sense of fear in the young about sexual consequences (masturbation causing blindness for example); now teachers of sex often lean over in the opposite direction and imply that no consequences will flow from sexual indulgence, when in fact they may.[6]

The question 'What am I becoming?' covers a far wider range of development than sex. Many of a boy's adventures, challenges, obstinacies, and originalities are probes towards the future, put into the field of this generalized doubt.

There are three levels implicit in the question:

1. What *am* I?   This suggests doubts about a child's acceptance by the community and ability to cope with the environment.
2. Becoming?   Questions about the emergent novel personality that is taking shape.
3. What sort of a person shall I be? This leads to long-range, often religious questions about ideals of conduct and the fulfilment of personality in others.

Motivation is the process by which this big doubt about the future and all the feelings that go with it, are gradually conceptualized. Adolescents will only occasionally speak about this for they are too much involved. Nevertheless the question underlies their feelings, their moods, and almost all that they do. When a boy progressively masters a new skill—say playing the piano or gymnastics—he is shaping his answer to the identity question. When he experiments with abstract painting or throws himself into a dramatic part he is exploring new forms and hitherto unrealized regions of feeling. Or when he accepts a new role of responsibility, learning, as he must, the art of being formal as well as friendly, he is trying new roles without abandoning old ones. The second part of the question (. . . becoming?) tends to be dominant with older teenagers just as the first part (what *am* I . . .?) dominates the earlier period.

These processes are rarely simple, and there is overlapping and interlocking. It is important to remember that skill and

[6] For a discussion of the influence of learning and cultural stimuli of sexual arousal see Derek Wright, 'Sex, instinct or appetite', *New Society*, no. 347 (1969). 'Human sex is sustained . . . more by stimuli the individual has learned . . . than by physiology.' See also F. A. Beach, 'Characteristics of the Masculine "Sex Drive" ' in the *Nebraska Symposium on Motivation*, 1956.

imagination have probably always developed hand in hand. I find it hard to resist the guess that the magic power of palaeolithic cave paintings was part of the psychological process of sharpening mental images—the conceptual counterpart of sharpening the external skills of hunting.[7] But one does not have to rely on such distant speculations. What of the boy whose life spins round fishing or round the less predatory love of wild birds? I have only to recall my passionate and vivid yearning for mountains in adolescence to taste something of this. It is rather like being in love; the strong, recurrent image is part of the process of motivation. Never decry the day-dreaming or doodling of a child. He is preparing for the hunt, in his own cave.

Consider the hunter—stone-age or teen-age, for some of the ground is common. When he can project a picture of his quarry and of its killing, not as a childish day-dream but realistically as part of the conceptual pattern of his skill, then it comes within the field of his potential action. Skill and symbol lie together in his mind. He is poised to kill, even though hours and days separate him from that bloody triumph. Of course the intelligent animal of prey is also possessed of many skills and is pushed by powerful appetites. Its knowledge of locality may be greater than the human hunter's but it has no conceptual picture of either terrain or quarry—no map and no motive.[8] Here is the gap which narrow behaviourism will never bridge.

The young hunter holds his desired object in mind night and day and all his actions become animated around imaginative activity which stretches before him into the future. This situation, in which the imagined goal is both shadowy and powerful, will be familiar to readers who have taken adventurous but responsible

[7] See G. R. Levy, *The Gate of Horn*, especially Chapter 2, 'The Religious Ideas Common to Modern Hunting Peoples', where she discusses the way in which an art and ritual have been used 'to raise the human group to such an intensity of shared action and emotion that it can create commensurate power'.

[8] Prof. W. H. Thorpe queries this phrase 'no map and no motive'. Though this is pure speculation it might be worth investigating whether the difference lies in man's ability to visualize two-dimensional pictures of places, whereas animals recall linear sequences, but cf. the Andean Culture, whose only 'maps' were strings with knots at intervals.

decisions in work or leisure. The symbolic goal may be more vague, like Columbus's Cathay, or more precise, like Hillary's image of Everest's final ridge, but there will always be a penumbra of uncertainty. And when the goal is reached the image evaporates. In retrospect it becomes precise, the thing itself. 'There was nothing to it really', says the hero. But without the imagination and the feelings to generate persistent, haunting symbols, I doubt if a man would take many of the risks his freedom offers.

In summary we can say that a man will sustain motivated behaviour when his feelings are directed to symbols whose referents, though vague, fall within the potential field generated by his emerging skills and concepts. The symbol does not refer to 'a goal', but to a unique field with many possibilities within it.

There is a continuum here which joins all conscious hopes: the hunter's quarry, the draftsman's blue print and even the mystic's vision. There are variables of scope and intensity but the shared elements are significant. Near one extreme, with vagueness and strong feelings prominent, is the primitive huntsman. His well-loved axe, his precious throwing spears, the memory of past encounters, his hungry family—all these contribute to his preparedness and at the centre is the flickering, powerful concept of a slain animal. No matter how skilled he is, the future is 'bigger' than all his calculations. It is full of hazards and incalculable elements, so there will be room for choice, error, and falling short. At the other extreme, consider an engineering designer. He too has been busy envisaging future contingencies, the dimensions of a strut perhaps, and how it will brace a loaded truss. He has drawn into his calculations much precision from science, but he too must recognize margins of error, the compromises and choices where his skill and freedom will interact with future events. There are strong feelings here too, less stirring than those of the hunter or the child, for an engineer's feelings are well channelled by training, professional codes, and routine. But they are what provide the energy for all his enterprise. On the engineer's desk there are pictures too—blue prints, critical-path analyses, and long-term plans, whose function is both to coordinate much calculation of materials, energy, time, and men and, by so doing, to expedite action.

The relationship in time between symbolic goal, skill, and achieved object brings out the asymmetry which we have observed earlier. It explains a phenomenon which parents and teachers often find annoying. Adolescents seem, sometimes, to be very obtuse in not appreciating the importance of qualifications and proper preparation for a career which is only a year or two away. The adolescent, too, may feel irritated and talk scathingly about 'the rat race' and 'materialist adults', yet still do nothing. This is the practical reflection of 'asymmetry', a deep misunderstanding which cannot be cleared up by mere discussion, for it results from seeing things from opposite time positions.

If we follow our customary technique of stretching this problem out in time its nature becomes clearer. Seen from beforehand a motive or future goal usually looks unreal, daunting, powerful perhaps, and vague; but seen from after its attainment it appears real, feasible, and precise. For this reason adults tend to talk about goals as though they were bull's eyes on a target, whereas, to the young, they look more like a dark shadow moving in the trees. It is better not to talk much about goals and motivation when this deep barrier exists; or if one must talk, to talk allusively. This explains why any effective education in the symbolic penetration of adult activities and in experiencing the feelings which these involve, is such an important field.

Consider a boy or girl who goes on an Outward Bound Course. Older people are inclined to nod their heads approvingly and say: 'Ah yes, character training—Splendid!' It may be splendid, but the word 'training' is a poor description of what is happening. The value of such experience lies not in the direction of hardening or of being prepared for some tough task but in this, that the teenager is discovering implicitly that he has unexpected potentialities. This truth hits him or her, not in words, not even in the earnings of badges, but in experience. The exploration is twofold: externally it involves new physical and aesthetic encounters— gale-force winds or water seen looking down through pine trees; internally there is an exploration of his or her own scope, in stoicism, resilience, stamina, and sensitivity. There are also discoveries made through people, encountered in new settings.

It is extremely difficult for secondary schools to educate this kind of awareness. They have limited time and few teachers. Narrow, arbitrary, attainable goals dominate the scene. The goals of examinations, of football and athletics can, undoubtedly, have real educational value, but they suffer from one big fault: they easily confuse our attitude towards work and achievement by their artificial precision. The indeterminacy and vagueness of real goals is an essential concomitant of freedom. A marriage, a career, a vocation have not been arranged. Yet out there on the plain, where a child's persistent self awaits him, causes and crowds will press as hard on his freedom as they do, today, on yours. Freedom waits in the future—undetermined, shadowy, but a powerful influence on today's young.

10   The old and the young

A leader is best
When people barely know that he exists,
Not so good when people obey and acclaim him,
Worst when they despise him.
'Fail to honour people,
They fail to honour you;'
But of a good leader who talks little,
When his work is done, his aim fulfilled,
They will say, 'we did it ourselves'.

LAOTZÜ, The Way of Life[1]

If we are to live in crowds—and this seems to be our destiny—we
need to deepen insight not only into ourselves and each other but
into the communities we belong to. Sometimes we seem to be
experiencing, in the crowded context of schools, lessons which
will be relevant to the dense habitats of the twenty-first century.

Here are three examples: talk, codes of behaviour, and mecha-
nization. One soon learns, in secondary schools today, that
discipline needs underpinning with a much more adequate structure of 'talk' than it did a generation ago. There are occasions, of
course, when orders must be obeyed unquestioningly; but these
are only likely to be survived without disruptive stress, if people
understand that in principle the instructions could be discussed—
at some appropriate time and place. The need for intensive communication is being more widely realized in industry and politics.
Formerly it applied to 'the few who knew'; now it applies to all.
Talk in this sense means genuine encounters between people, with
silence, searching, and perplexity, as well as information, tying
them together.

Another example is provided by codes of conduct. There has
been a curious sentiment at work in school and society which
equates progressiveness with the absence of law. In one sense this

---

[1] Translated by Witter Brynner (Poetry London, 1946).

is justified. If a person makes progress in a skill, he allows the initiatory system of rules and maxims to sink into his unconscious memory and he can then exploit the freedom with which this internalized order endows him. This kind of experience by individuals may have led to the widespread, but absurd, assumption that schools and other communities should aim at out growing codes. I have met an example, in a College of Education, where students yearn for clear elementary guidance in classroom procedures. But, to quote one of these, 'the staff seem conscientiously to avoid giving tips that might be helpful because it would reek of formal methods'. The truth is, not that we should eliminate such formal procedures, but that people in schools should become more aware of the initiatory and skeletal function of codes. For these are like proteins—hard to synthesize, hard to assimilate, but structurally useful. In society it is people who have earned authority, those who do things well and know how they do things well, who must be responsible for making and changing codes. In schools I do not think there is a rational case for involving children in major law-making decisions; there is a very strong case for letting them feel, much more readily, the pressures and possibilities which surround the process. School councils which pretend to be functioning as democratic bodies can be a source of great frustration and boredom, just because in most matters they can not be decision-taking arenas. There may be a case, sometimes, for clearly limited areas of experimental self-government; but it should be seen for what it is—a kind of play, though it can be called by a bigger name. Even staff meetings will lose in quality if they aim at democratic action. Their concern is something more subtle. A council of senior children, and even more a staff meeting, can periodically become a crucible for the refinement of problems, for relating these to first principles, and for sketching out a range of possible solutions. It is sometimes in a community's interest to agonize over a problem for months or years; at other times a quick decision, taken by the head under a sense of crisis, can be discussed and analysed retrospectively—and modified. If these processes, which are far more concerned with information and imagination than with power, are gone through adequately, few members of the community will resent the fact that someone—usually the headmaster or headmistress—has got to take a decision. The heat should be generated round the problem, not round the decision.

My third example links the first and second. People often say that mechanical improvements in education (teaching machines for example) are acceptable, provided that they are used to release teachers for the kind of work they do best. Doubtless this is true, but it leaves open the question of what is the work that people do best when freed by machines. It is not more leisure, or more knowledge, or more democracy, or more change that machines might provide time for in schools. All these have their place, but none will be effective without more unhurried contact between old and young in the context of small groups.

In this chapter we shall be mainly concerned with that simplest but scarce commodity, the essential relationship which exists between one younger and one older person. I still recall, as a six-year-old child, hearing my elder brother use that magic syllable 'let's . . .' when some afternoon exploit was afoot. In those four letters are concentrated the essence of education: its adventure, its freedom, its shared but vague objectives, and the joint endeavour of the young and the less young.

If we could understand more fully how this 'joint psychology' works, uniting teacher and pupil in a shared aim, we might build educational thought on a firmer basis. Is not this the fundamental unit, the basic coupling, from which theory should grow?

But because such teacher/pupil situations are generally of brief duration, or are diluted out of all recognition by large numbers in schools, they are difficult to isolate and treat scientifically. One does experience them in small teaching groups, in tutorials which are not hurried, and when coaching physical skills. Such couplings are also not infrequently met in counselling situations, when an experienced tutor or housemaster becomes involved, for quite long periods, in a therapeutic clinch, with some wayward boy or girl.

As we move down the scale, from large groups to small, we are moving away from the level of objective social science, where statistics and general rules may be important, to a level where we must be deeply involved and, for a while, must diminish our objectivity. At the same time our concern shifts from considering what has happened (and may be analysed) to the field of what might happen (and may be symbolized). So we come to reflect on the meanings of people, the 'more' which might emerge in future from the present 'less'. It is as though two climbers of differing experience and capacity were scaling a steep ridge, looking up towards unknown difficulties. The future of the enterprise depends not only on synchronous action but even more on shared objectives and shared trust.

WHAT MEANING DO WE SEE IN THEM?

The child knows in his bones it is *hope* that is locked up in the wicked behaviour, and that *despair* is linked with compliance and false socialization (D. W. Winnicott).[2]

The nature of the dialogue between older and younger people is certainly something of a mystery. We understand a good deal about the transfer of trivial information—the sort of teaching simple machines could do—but we know little about the transfer of emotions, attitudes, and aspirations. In the examples that follow we shall again encounter the asymmetry of the relationship—'They don't see us the way we see them.' 'Our way' (that of adults') inevitably tends to be coloured by our wider experience and our capacity for analysing; 'their way' inevitably tends towards feeling and symbolism.

My first fictitious but familiar example is Jim (aged 12), who has just been caught smoking. This is contrary to the rules of his school and it is the third offence in a month. He will have to be punished. But this will solve nothing, and it will not free the teachers concerned with Jim from feeling (not for the first time) both flouted and frustrated. They can ease the weight of these feelings a little by recapitulating some of the causes which lie beyond their control: the boy's sense of insecurity in regard to

[2] 'The Young Child at Home and School' from *Moral Education in a Changing Society*, ed. W. R. Niblett (Faber, 1963).

his father, his anxious chain-smoking mother, etc. These help to explain Jim's intransigence. But we often need to go further than this and to feel how the offender feels. We need to suffer something of the claustrophobia of school routine, to feel Jim's yearning for urgent, youthful freedom, and to share the thrill (cheap but real) of slipping over the stile behind the gymnasium and of escaping up into the woods. And we need to share the not-so-cheap pleasure of lying back in silence and looking at the space of sky in green tracery and of then—with mature skill—blowing smoke rings. Further, I think we must admit that this may be as much a spiritual experience for Jim as a communion service or a Quaker silence or a symphony might be for us. For Jim, at this particular stage, these minutes may have been the nearest he could get to the ultimate meaning of life. Such reflections may not, alas, stop us from punishing him, though they may, a little, alter our manner of doing so. I have perhaps over-emphasized the poetry of this small action of revolt; but it is always better to err in the direction of seeing too much meaning in the free acts of children than too little.

If you asked Jim what his action meant the answer would probably be a blank stare, veiling his view that you were a nut case. But if, in thirty years, Jim could look back on his youth, though much of his experience might appear dim and mechanical, he would see in this grey ocean a chain of sun-lit islands, which were those scattered times when he felt free, happy, human, and himself. It is the vague anticipation of such moments that gives some meaning and purpose to the often painful business of growing up. If Jim or Jane ever envisage this sun-lit archipelago their symbolism may be a little naïve—pop stars, Lotus cars, and probably love-making. Such hedonism may seem to adults a little restricted, but for the young, without the groundwork of such simple hopes, no seeds will grow.

It is not merely in isolation and revolt that children dig the soil of their freedom. More important, though less spectacular, are the situations where skills and attitudes are transmitted from parent to child, from master to apprentice. When this happens it is always in the context of a shared aim. But, as we have seen, distant aims which seem obvious and powerful to an adult may have no value at all to the child. For the daughter who 'can't decide about her future', discussion may be useless; but if mother and daughter get down to the job of converting that stewing steak into a convincing goulash, they will at least exercise their joint ingenuity. It is this kind of activity which generates the field where motives form. The skilled teacher is constantly opening up small avenues of search, of inquiry, of paradox and problem, which he shares with his pupils. This almost always involves a withdrawal of his own assertiveness. He doesn't withdraw his judgement—that is always available; or his sense of truth—that he shares. He waits. He says, 'O.K., what are you (or we) going to do about it?' In the space so created the joint experience of skill, the judgement of success or failure, and the authority of truth do their own work. This, or something like it, was the creative gift of which Keats spoke when he coined that most unpoetic phrase 'negative capability'.[3] To exert this kind of subtle skill requires great confidence, not so much in oneself as in the process of learning, and it demands faith in the child.

Our vision of what a child might become is vitally important, but it should be a private, hopeful, tentative affair. It is not our business as parent or teacher to start furnishing or narrowing this field of motivation, though occasionally a well-timed jolt may do no harm. A reasonably gifted and stable child gradually becomes aware of the possibilities that lie ahead of him. But what of the less able or disturbed child? It is tempting for us to imagine nothing, to shrug our shoulders with pessimistic realism. This may be a serious mistake. True, the scales may appear to be weighted against 'success'. But what is success? What of our own past follies and near escapes? What of the 'less able' men and women who befriended us as children? What strange developments in poetry, courage, and even sanctity might flow from this grubby source? To believe in unpromising children is partly to confess our own ignorance; but it is also an imaginative act. These

---

[3] 'Negative Capability, that is, when a man is capable of being in uncertainties, mysteries, doubts, without any irritable reaching after fact and reason' John Keats, *Letters to G. and T. Keats*, 21 Dec. 1817.

thoughts need not often be expressed; but they can be deployed in such a way as to upset the dull machinery of probability.

Does this mean that a teacher to be effective must be a vague, negative optimist who just keeps silent, questions, trusts? I don't think this follows; because most successful teachers are noisy enough and extroverted enough already. But they sometimes fail to explore the subtler ways of poetry and the *Tao*.

WHAT MEANING DO THEY SEE IN US?

I have a housemaster in mind, again a composite fiction. Let us call him Mr. Brown. His skill in human dealings is largely practical. He is not prejudiced against psychology, neither is he much interested in it or in theories about people. He is interested in children—his own family and the children in his care. Most schools have their problem children; and most, fortunately, have some teachers with the gift of getting the best from them. Mr. Brown was one of these.

John was one of the problems. At the age of eleven he entered Mr. Brown's house. Within a week he was suspected of slitting the tyres of one of his 'enemies'. (Later a list was found.) Within a month other destructive and vindictive incidents were proved. Headmaster and housemaster gradually extended their picture of the boy and his background. They had met the parents, a conventional and serious-minded pair who worked abroad. But it now became apparent from correspondence that the father was a rigid perfectionist, who claimed to have overcome the difficulties of his own childhood by the exercise of traditional British virtues. Mr. Brown guessed from other clues that the mother had learned, long ago, to button up most of her emotions and to display a correspondingly austere front.

These mental portraits of John's parents were provisional and shadowy in Mr. Brown's mind. But his picture of their son was clear and discouraging. In addition to vandalism John was beginning to show powers of leadership, and these were almost always in the wrong direction. With other members of staff, especially with one rather insecure science master, the relationship was characterized by calculating truculence, on the one hand, and on the other by thinly concealed fear and disciplinary deadlock. The headmaster usually arranged that Mr. Brown, rather than himself, would deal with the periodic crises which emerged. But there were a few signs of hope. Though John was ready to lie, more or less on principle, he showed, in argument, a respect for truth, and he could sometimes see a joke. He had also taken a liking to Mrs. Brown. These were small shreds of comfort for the hard-pressed Mr. Brown. Then one or two parents of other children began to complain . . .

This kind of situation will not be entirely unfamiliar to secondary teachers. I have sketched it, not to evoke sympathy in the reader's mind, but as a reminder that this kind of situation is extremely common. We need to pause more and to understand what is going on all round us. Mr. Brown does not say: 'My boy, behind the mask I recognize great possibilities . . .' He sees more than he can readily formulate in words and then *acts* on what he sees.

Mr. Brown's actions might give the casual observer an impression of inconsistency and inconsequence. He is often too busy—genuinely busy. Sometimes he will be very outspoken and occasionally angry (but angry about happenings rather than *with* John), sometimes he will enjoy the boy's conversation, sometimes he will be withdrawn, often he will do nothing and just wait. If there are punishments they must be as impersonal as possible and with no nagging. To his colleagues and headmaster Mr. Brown advocates restraint and patience. If any of his actions are at the level of calculated manœuvring, no good will come. But as long as there is firm ground beneath the flickering surface, John will discover it.

Most teenagers are perceptive, practical psychologists; disturbed ones are especially penetrating. What does John see? He realizes that he has come up against a somewhat complicated character. But from early encounters he has sensed that Mr. Brown is not a phoney—not much anyway. John's own emotional attitude swings constantly and colours what he sees. Liking, hatred, a desire to score victories, black depression, and perplexity succeed each other and rarely last long. But through this shifting screen of contact and over a period of years, John's attitude gradually centres on a concept which is really too big for him and which had never entered his mind before—something to do with manhood and the man he might become.

It is important to see the contrast between these two viewpoints. Mr. Brown's attitude to John is characterized at first by a piecemeal knowledge which provides him with the raw material for building up a vague but hopeful view of the boy's possibilities. Feelings of positive liking may only grow slowly. He is an artist. John's view of his housemaster, on the other hand, will probably be strongly charged with feeling from the beginning. Only much later will precepts of behaviour and analysis of conduct become related to the remembered father-figure. Then, as mature analysis takes the place of confused and partial insight, the young man may feel some compassion for the declining Mr. Chips and may appreciate some of the pressures, wounds, failures, and successes which went to make that life. Or he may never give him another thought.

If this picture of asymmetrical relationship is roughly true an important point begins to emerge. Mr. Brown appeared to John as an object of feeling and emotion. Understanding him by reason and analysis are many years away. We have seen that it is mainly through symbols that new truths enter our minds. For the child's rapidly expanding horizon this is particularly true; the windows are narrower and the bars thicker for adolescents, but they are not shut. The father figure is slowly assimilated as a symbol of . . . what? Not of some abstract good I think, but of John's own future manhood.[4]

In one sense this may be obvious. It could be said: 'Of course adults are templates around which the habits of children are formed.' But this is far too mechanical a model. It implies a pliability and servility in the young which are far from the truth. The symbol, on the other hand, foreshadows a field of meaning

[4] I read Jerome S. Bruner's *Toward a Theory of Instruction* only after completing this book. Many of his ideas are extremely relevant to this chapter. He refers to the kind of human symbol which I have in mind here as 'competence models' (pp. 123 and 125).

whose reference is mainly in the future; for John it is an existential meaning, which he feels and experiences but cannot name. He sees himself and his own freedom darkly through this sympathetic adult.

In many other, simpler cultures children grew and were initiated into a world well provided with symbols of manhood and womanhood. But today the ritual and the folk-lore are thin. The young enjoy the far-out disc jockey or this year's fashion model, but they soon see the sterility which lies behind. Now it is mainly people, stripped of all regalia, who must mediate meaning. To proclaim the message often weakens it; a man and a woman are their message and their meaning lies beyond them, partly in the future.

11 Doubt

All truth is shadow except the last, except the utmost; yet every
truth is true in its kind. It is substance in its own place, though it be
but a shadow in another place.

ISAAC PENNINGTON[1]

In this book many questions have been suggested, certainly more
than have been answered. Can our educational communities
become places where truth and purpose grow without stifling
individuality? Can we teach anybody to be creative? What is the
role of ritual and symbol in all this? Can we educate ourselves—
teachers and parents—to seek more patiently the long-term significance of all that happens? Can we develop new concepts of
education, concepts which proclaim the wholeness, uniqueness,
and freedom of people? And new concepts of order and responsibility? Even though we have no prophetic vision to offer, can we
prepare the ground for coming generations to be sensitive in the
rediscovery of wonder and worship?

Such questions throw our inquiring gaze beyond short-term
educational aims like 'the good citizen' of 'the well-adjusted
group', towards more remote and puzzling vistas. We have con-
sidered briefly the conceptual changes that happen in a child's
mind as he grows through adolescence to maturity. But what of
the new concepts which may now be changing our own minds?
Are we teachers clinging to vague, 'progressive' formulae which
may have been relevant and fresh in the nineteen-thirties, but are
not now? There is always a time-lag between the development
of new philosophical or psychological concepts and their widespread influence; first come the years of liberation, then, too
often, the crusty hang-over.

[1] Isaac Pennington, an early Quaker (1616–79). These words of his are
on the flyleaf of *Christian Faith and Practice*, the 'official' anthology of
the Society of Friends.

There are indications that we, in the West, are approaching a period of revolutionary educational re-thinking. The questions that are beginning to loom up are very big ones—big and ancient. They do not fit into the now meaningless frame which equates 'good' and 'progressive' and 'permissive'. The writers we have been reconnoitring in this book seem to throw light on the kind of journey that lies ahead. There are other witnesses too, in the fields of anthropology, ethology, cybernetics, and linguistics who reinforce them. They all seem to be telling us to take a more searching look at the psalmist's question: 'What is man . . . that Thou . . . art Mindful . . . of him?' The search is for a more universal sense of order. It spans all narrow cultural divisions and reaches out to the distant past and distant future. One suddenly comes on surprising examples: Norbet Wiener produces the idea that St. Augustine's concept of evil as *incompleteness* is comparable to the physicist's concept of entropy (dis-order), while Manichaean evil, a positive and malicious force, is not;[2] William Thorpe claims that the perceptive imagination of an artist will be as necessary to future scientists as deductive and experimental prowess;[3] Konrad Lorenz stresses that our basic patterns of perception are as much inherited as the fins of a fish;[4] and Levi-Strauss the anthropologist defies convention by seeking for the genetically transmitted 'structures', running through all mankind, which help to determine the patterns of primitive kinship, art, and myth.[5] They are all drilling down towards universals.

Even more rewarding may be the prospecting that is going on in linguistics. Noam Chomsky has discovered, with apparently rigorous analysis and observation, that the patterns of all speech are underlain by archetypal forms—'generative grammar'—which is shared by the whole human race, and that learning a language

[2] *The Human use of Human Beings*, pp. 14, 15.
[3] 'Vitalism and Organicism' from *The Uniqueness of Man*, p. 96.
[4] Noam Chomsky gives details of this early (1941) remark of Lorenz's on p. 88 of *Language and Mind*.
[5] Claude Levi-Strauss, *Structural Anthropology*. But the present fashion for wild 'structuralist' speculation in France should be a warning against uncritical enthusiasm. See Roger Poole, 'Structuralism Sidetracked', in *New Blackfriars*, July 1969.

happens 'on top' of these patterns, developing, modifying, but not erasing them. He castigates the behaviourist psychologists, rather in the manner of Elijah on Mount Carmel urging the prophets of Baal to keep trying. 'Even today', writes Chomsky, 'the task [of determining the hereditary principles which shape our mental functioning] remains for the future. It is a task that need not be undertaken if the empiricist psychological doctrine can be substantiated; therefore it is of great importance to subject this doctrine to rational analysis, as has been done, in part, in the study of linguistics.'[6]

Some of these speculations will almost certainly go wide of the mark. Nevertheless the message to us of such explorations outside the field of conventional educational thinking seems to be: *look deeper*. We should remember that in the terms that we have been developing this phrase 'look deeper' is a convenient spatial metaphor telling us to use imagination, to form new images which unite formerly diverse or conflicting patterns of perception as we reflect on man and mind. It is the splendid, emergent, incomplete phenomenon of man which confronts us with our greatest tasks—tasks in which religion, art, and science are complementary, tasks which can only be undertaken within symbolic frames transcending us and our present communities.

The patterns of these communities will change more in the next century than we can begin to imagine. They may move in the direction of chaos, of intense smaller groupings, or of new world-wide consciousness—or of all of these and others. Because of this flux of change and the rising tide of information which engulfs us, teachers are already confronting a heroic task. It is sometimes suggested that the essential and primary part of this is the rediscovery of values. I do not think so.

If we were to follow this thread far it would lead us into an interesting field beyond the scope of this book. But consider it for

[6] Chomsky, *Language and Mind*, p. 79. Strong criticism of the behaviourist psychologists will also be found in the preface. My own reaction to this contest is partly the enjoyment of someone else's combat, but it is also coloured by the feeling that too much of our teacher training is affected by the extreme assumptions of behaviourism and empiricism and that a reaction is overdue.

a moment. The idea of values as handy and distinct tests, with which one can agree or disagree, is attractive, but it lacks energy. Are not values always the unsought profit from endeavours directed elsewhere? They are like the rules of art which look familiar and right after we have mastered the art, but beforehand they seem arbitrary and unattractive. If our art happens to be a game like week-end sketching or squash we can pick up the rules on Saturday and drop them on Monday. Values differ from these rules in that they are integral, not optional, equipment. They are part of an all-embracing commitment, and though this may not be very effective or consistent it is, nevertheless, held together by what Polanyi calls 'a universal intent'. This means an individual person's continuing effort towards action and under-standing unified by truth. It is *such* endeavours that will recreate values.

Big words! But they need not imply a dogmatic uniformity. If a person's values are integral to his own sustained effort and part of his total competence, there is no contradiction in saying that the values are absolute for him and yet that still there may come a stage in which he could transcend them. He is still subject to change, but not piecemeal change, rather the total evolutionary or revolutionary change which would affect his whole way of life. At such metamorphoses the older values will not be scrapped but reintegrated in a wider scheme.[7] So I do not think we should be very conscious of our values; though, like respectable friends, they are helpful in a crisis and can be sharp-tongued critics.

In the business of education doubt is our most constant com-panion, one with whom we need to come to terms. Doubt is not very far away when any new endeavour is afoot and it is the background to our hopes and an ingredient in our faith. We may try to eliminate it from our machines, but never from our labora-tories, our workshops, or our libraries. Imagine how full of doubt the teacher is the day before school starts. The corridors echo with hygienic menace. But we come to appreciate even these

[7] For a penetrating criticism of 'situation ethics' and the need for a proper understanding of revolutionary change see Herbert McCabe, *Law, Love and Language*, Chapters 1 and 2.

cavernous moods, for after all, tomorrow there will be children filling these ordered times and spaces, children with names. Routine, like sleep, is precious; but in action we need to treat it a little lightly, to reject the idols of certainty and keep turning our imagination towards the margins of numinous doubt. That is where the skilled work starts.

Bibliography

ABERCROMBIE, M. L. J., *The anatomy of judgment* (Hutchinson, London, 1960).

ARENDT, HANNAH, *The human condition* (University of Chicago Press, 1958).

AUGUSTINE, SAINT, *The confessions*, translated by F. J. Sheed (Sheed & Ward, London, 1945).

BARBOUR, IAN L. G., *Issues in science and religion* (Student Christian Movement, London, 1966). A comprehensive and clear survey of this frontier. The author is a physicist with wide knowledge of current theological and philosophical problems. His own view favours the process philosophy stemming from Whitehead.

BATESON, GREGORY, 'Conscious Purpose versus Nature' in *The dialectics of liberation* (Penguin Books, London, 1968).

BINDRA, D., and STEWART, J., eds., *Motivation* (Penguin Books, London, 1966).

BRAIN, W. RUSSELL, *Mind, perception and science* (Blackwell, Oxford, 1951).

BRONOWSKI, J., *The identity of man* (Heinemann, London, 1966).

—— *Insight* (Macdonald, London, 1964).

BRUNER, JEROME S., *The process of education* (Vintage Books, 1960).

—— *Toward a theory of instruction* (Harvard University Press, 1967). His ideas have been developed in connection with work on curriculum reform and with backward children and bear closely on the theme of this book.

BUBER, M., *I and thou* (T. & T. Clark, Edinburgh, 1937).

—— *Between man and man* (Kegan Paul, Trench & Trubner, 1947, and Fontana Books). This includes his essay on education which influenced Herbert Read.

CAMERON, H. C., *Sir Joseph Banks, the aristocrat of the philosophers* (Batchworth Press, London, 1952).

CASSIRER, ERNST, *Language and myth*, translated by Susanne K. Langer (Dover Books, 1953).

—— *An essay on man* (Yale University Press, New Haven, 1944).

CHOMSKY, N., *Language and mind* (Harcourt, Brace & World, New York, 1968). Here, in three essays, he summarizes his views on linguistic research. The central chapter is difficult and highly theoretical but the others are straightforward; all are of great interest.

CLARK, SIR KENNETH, 'The Blot and the Diagram' in *Encounter*, January 1963.

COLERIDGE, S. T. (The Penguin Poets, London, 1957). This anthology, edited by Kathleen Raine, is an excellent source for the non-specialist.

COPLESTON, F. C., *Aquinas* (Penguin Books, London, 1955). A clear, concise introduction to Thomist and some Aristotelian ideas.

DIAMOND, E., *The science of dreams* (Eyre & Spottiswoode, London, 1962).

ELIOT, GEORGE. Quotations are from the Zodiac edition of *Middlemarch* and the Everyman edition of *Felix Holt*.

FREUD, S., *The interpretation of dreams*, parts 1 and 2 (The Hogarth Press, London, 1953).

Friends, Society of, *Christian faith and practice in the experience of the Society of Friends* (Friends Book Centre, London, 1960).

GODIN, A., ed., *From cry to word: contributions towards a psychology of prayer* (Lumen Vitae Press, Brussels, 1968). I have not read this. It was reviewed in *New Blackfriars*, February 1969, by Dorothy Berridge.

GRENE, MARJORIE, *A portrait of Aristotle* (Faber, London, 1963).
—— *The knower and the known* (Faber, London, 1966).
　　Her books form an interesting bridge between classical philosophy, biology, and existentialism.

GOMBRICH, E. H., *Art and illusion* (Phaidon, London, 1960).

GOODMAN, NELSON, *The languages of art* (O.U.P., 1969).

HAIGHT, G. S., *George Eliot, a biography* (O.U.P., 1968).

HARDY, ALISTAIR, *The living stream* (Collins, London, 1965).

HUDSON, LIAM, *Contrary imaginations* (Methuen, London, 1966). One of the most readable and useful books on education.
—— *Frames of mind* (Methuen, London, 1968).

HUXLEY, JULIAN, ed., *The humanist frame* (George Allen & Unwin, London, 1961).

JUNG, C. G., *Contributions to analytical psychology* (Kegan Paul, Trench & Trubner, London, 1928).
—— *Modern man in search of a soul* (Kegan Paul, Trench & Trubner, London, 1933). See also WILHELM and JUNG.
　　These books are a good introduction, and show more clearly than some books about Jung how he is often at pains not to introduce dualist, transcendent concepts into psychology.

KAPP, R. O., *Mind, life and body* (Constable, London, 1951).

KELLER, HELEN, *The story of my life* (Hodder & Stoughton, London, 1907).

KOESTLER, ARTHUR, *Insight and outlook* (Macmillan, London, 1947).
—— *The sleepwalkers* (Hutchinson, London, 1959).
—— *The act of creation* (Hutchinson, London, 1964).

KUHN, THOMAS S., *The structure of scientific revolutions* (The University of Chicago Press, 1961).

H

LANGER, SUSANNE K., *Philosophy in a new key, a study in the symbolism of reason, rite and art* (Harvard University Press, Cambridge, Mass., 1957). First published in 1942; in this third edition Professor Langer clears up some sign/signal confusion.

—— *Philosophical sketches* (O.U.P., London, 1962). Here she develops her definition of a symbol.

—— *Mind, an essay on human feeling* (Johns Hopkins Press, Baltimore, 1967). This is the first volume of her attempt at a major synthesis.

LANGFORD, G., *Philosophy and education* (Macmillan, London, 1968).

LAOTZÜ, *The way of life*, translated by Walter Bynner (Poetry London, London, 1946).

LEVI-STRAUSS, CLAUDE, *Structural anthropology* (Allen Lane, The Penguin Press, London, 1968).

LEVY, G. R., *The gate of horn* (Faber, London, 1948).

LORENZ, K., *King Solomon's ring* (Methuen, London, 1953).

—— *On aggression* (Methuen, London, 1966). It may be that some of his popularizers (e.g. Robert Ardrey) read too much into Lorenz's interpretation of man's biological aggressiveness.

LURIA, A. R., and YUDOVICH, F., *Speech and the development of mental processes in the child* (Staples, London, 1959).

McCABE, HERBERT, *Law, love and language* (Sheed & Ward, London, 1968).

MACKAY, D. M., *Christianity in a mechanistic universe and other essays* (ed. MacKay, Inter-Varsity Fellowship, London, 1965).

—— 'On the Logical Indeterminacy of Free Choice', *Mind*, N.S. lxix (1960), no. 273.

—— *Freedom of action in a mechanistic universe* (C.U.P., 1967).

McLUHAN, MARSHALL, *The Gutenberg galaxy* (Routledge & Kegan Paul, 1962).

—— *Understanding media* (Routledge & Kegan Paul, London, 1964). The former conveys McLuhan's main ideas; the latter is more what he calls a 'do it yourself kit'. *The Penguin McLuhan* contains some good articles about him.

MALINOWSKI, B., *The foundations of faith and morals* (O.U.P., 1936).

MASCALL, E. L., *Words and images* (Longmans, London, 1957). Ch. IV, 'The Two Ideals of Knowledge', is relevant to the first three chapters of this book and gives a theological context to them.

NIBLETT, W. R., ed., *Moral education in a changing society* (Faber, London, 1963). This contains D. W. Winnicott's essay.

NOYCE, W., and SUTTON, G., *Samson, the life and writings of Menlove Edwards* (Cloister Press).

O'CONNOR, K., *Learning, an introduction* (Macmillan, London, 1968).

ORIGEN, *De principiis (On first principles)* (Everyman).

OSWALD, I., *Sleep* (Penguin Books, London, 1966).

PETERS, R. S., *The concept of motivation* (Routledge & Kegan Paul, London, 1958).

—— 'Education as Initiation', a contribution to *Philosophical analysis and education*, ed. R. D. Archambault (Routledge & Kegan Paul, London, 1965).

PIAGET, J., *The language and thought of a child* (Geneve, 1926; Routledge & Kegan Paul, London, 1959).

—— *The child's conception of numbers* (Geneva, 1941; Routledge & Kegan Paul, London, 1952).

POLANYI, MICHAEL, *Personal knowledge* (Routledge & Kegan Paul, London, 1958).

—— *The tacit dimension* (Routledge & Kegan Paul, London, 1966).

—— *Knowing and being* (Routledge & Kegan Paul, London, 1969).

POTTER, S., *The theory and practice of gamesmanship* (Hart-Davis, London, 1947).

RAINE, KATHLEEN, *Defending ancient springs* (O.U.P., 1967).

READ, HERBERT, *Education through art* (Faber, London, 1945).

RYLE, G., *The concept of mind* (Hutchinson, London, 1949, Peregrine paper-back). This contains the famous 'Ghost in the Machine' discussion, a contemporary philosopher's case against dualism. Chapter VI on 'Self-knowledge' is relevant to this book. In some respects it opens the way to Polanyi's more dynamic accounts of self-knowing.

SARTRE, J. P., *Existentialism and humanism* (Methuen, London, 1948).

SEWELL, E., *The field of nonsense* (Chatto, London, 1952).

—— *The Orphic voice* (Routledge & Kegan Paul, London, 1960). This book is difficult but often interesting.

SHERRINGTON, CHARLES, *Man on his nature* (Pelican 1955, first published 1940).

SHRÖDINGER, E., *What is life?* (C.U.P., 1944).

—— *My view of the world* (C.U.P., 1964).
  The former was written nearly a decade before the discovery of DNA but is still interesting and relevant. He uses artistic symbols for the gene substance which was soon to be discovered.

STRAWSON, P. F., ed., *Studies in the philosophy of thought and action* (O.U.P., 1968).

TEILHARD DE CHARDIN, *The phenomenon of man* (Collins, London, 1959). There are many other books by and about him, but this contains his key ideas. He attracts needless contumely by claiming to be writing science. Though his groundwork is scientific, he builds up a symbolic edifice on this which is not scientific in any ordinary sense of the word; it is, nevertheless, a powerful and prophetic book.

THOMPSON, D'ARCY, *On growth and form* (abridged, C.U.P., 1961).

THORPE, W. H., *Learning and instinct in animals* (Methuen, London, 1956).

—— 'Ethology and Consciousness', Ch. 19 of *Brain and conscious experience* (ed. John C. Eccles, Springer Verlag, New York, 1966).

—— *The uniqueness of man*, ed Roslansky (North Holland, Amsterdam, 1969).

VYGOTSKY, L. S., *Thought and language* (M.I.T., 1962).

WADDINGTON, C. H., ed., *Towards a theoretical biology*, 2 vols. (Edinburgh University Press, 1968, 1969).

WAISSMANN, F., 'Language Strata', an essay in *Logic and language*, 2nd series, ed. A. G. N. Flew (Blackwell, Oxford, 1953) .

WHITEHEAD, A. N., *Process and reality* (Macmillan, London, 1929); a very difficult book.

—— *Symbolism* (C.U.P., 1927).

—— *Modes of thought* (C.U.P., 1935).

—— *The aims of education* (Williams & Norgate, London, 1932).

WHYTE, L. LAW, *The unconscious before Freud* (Tavistock, London, 1962).

WIENER, NORBERT, *The human use of human beings* (Houghton Mifflin, New York, 1950; Sphere Books, 1958); an abbreviation of his *Cybernetics*.

WILHELM, R., *The secret of the golden flower* (Routledge & Kegan Paul, London, 1931). Introduction and commentary by C. G. Jung.

WITTGENSTEIN, LUDWIG, *Philosophical investigations* (Blackwell, Oxford, 1968).

Index

PRINTED IN GREAT BRITAIN
AT THE UNIVERSITY PRESS, OXFORD
BY VIVIAN RIDLER
PRINTER TO THE UNIVERSITY